SPAS

Spas

The Cultural Economy of Hospitality, Magic and the Senses

Tom O'Dell

NORDIC ACADEMIC PRESS

Nordic Academic Press
P.O. Box 1206
S-221 05 Lund, Sweden
info@nordicacademicpress.com
www.nordicacademicpress.com

Typesetting: Stilbildarna i Mölle, Frederic Täckström
Cover: Jacob Wiberg
Cover image: Japanese outdoor pool at Hassel-
udden Spa, Stockholm. Photo: Tom O'Dell
Print: Livonia Print, Riga, Latvia 2010
ISBN: 978-91-85509-35-5

Contents

Acknowledgements   7

1. Spas   9
   The cultural economy   11
   The rise of the ephemeral   16
   The spas   20
   The organization of the book   25

2. Spas and the Shifting Context of Conditional Hospitality   27
   Hospitality: rights and obligations   29
   Private spaces and ulterior motives   33
   Hospital -ity   35
   Leisure and the opening of hospitable spaces   39
   Commercializing hospitality   42
   Demise and rebirth   50

3. Magic, Ritual, and the Mass Production of Serenity   53
   A general theory of magic   57
   Profane openings into the realm of rejuvenation   58
   Promising the impossible?   62
   The materiality of spell-casting: making sanctuaries   64
   Magical rites and production *ex nihilo*   72
   Floating rites   80
   Magical representations   82
   But is it really magic?   88

4. Spa Sensibilities   93
   Emotion, culture, and corporeality   95
   Material culture and sensual communication   98
   Organizational space and mobile bodies   106
   Hospitality and invisibility   118

5. Bringing the Spa Home   121
    Sensescaping the home   124
    More than hygiene   127
    Bigger, bubblier, and better   129
    Back to nature   131
    Enter the stranger   136

Notes   145

References   153

Acknowledgements

One of the most enjoyable aspects of being an ethnologist lies in the fact that in the course of your job you have the opportunity to meet people in spheres of daily life who you might otherwise never come in contact with. As I explain in the introduction to this book, I more or less stumbled into the world of spas. It was an employee of a large hotel chain who, at the end of an open lecture I held on the experience economy, approached me and asked me if I could hold a keynote speech at a coming international spa conference. I replied that I would be pleased to do so, but that I was unable to speak about spas specifically, since I had never been to one. The woman before me smiled and reassured me by saying, 'I can arrange for that.'

Over the coming years I spent many hours speaking with the managers, personnel, and patrons of spas. I would like to thank everyone who took the time to speak with me. Time and time again I was met by busy managers who explained that they only had a small amount of time to offer me, but more often than not I found myself sitting with them for an hour or two, listening to them explain how they had built up their facilities, how they overcame the problems they encountered, and how they envisioned the future. Books, ledgers, and digital accounting systems were opened to me as they explained the work required to run a spa. In some cases, managers booked me into their spas so that I could get a first-hand impression of what they were trying to explain to me. They introduced me to their staff and told them to answer whatever questions I had. And they did so. For this I would like to thank all of you.

The work of producing this book was not limited to just this field. Quite a few people read and commented upon various drafts to texts that ultimately came to be the cornerstones upon which this book is built. For this I would like to thank Peter Billing, Erika

Andersson Cederholm, Richard Ek, Sarah Gibson, Szilvia Gyimóthy, Johan Hultman, Orvar Löfgren, Jennie Germann Molz, Can Seng Ooi, and Robert Willim. Invaluable comments on the full-length manuscript of the book were provided by Johan Hultman, Orvar Löfgren, Robert Willim, and Lynn Åkesson.

To my wife Lotta Leo, thank you very much for your love and support. While most couples at the spas we visited cuddled and framed their visit as a time to be together, 'just the two of us', you had to put up with a husband who ran around taking pictures, and making notes. It was the kind of behavior that could almost make everyday life seem highly romantic in comparison. I promise, if we ever go to a spa again, the notebook will be left at home.

The research that this book is based upon was funded by a grant from the Swedish Research Council (*Vetenskapsrådet*). Funding for the publication and production of this book was provided by the Swedish Research Council and by *Nordenstedtska stiftelsen*.

— ❀ —

TO

MATILDA

CHAPTER I

Spas

The Cultural Economy of Hospitality, Magic, and the Senses

> We take care of the whole of you. A sense of well-being is felt as much in the soul as in the body. At Varberg Kurort, we have a holistic approach to health and we will be happy to support you if you wish to change or improve your lifestyle.
>
> (*Varbergs Kurort* brochure 2006: 12)

In the early summer of 2003 *Businessweek* carried an article with devastating news for the tourist industry. The combined effects of bad weather, unemployment, and the threat of terrorist attacks had contributed to a situation in which 54 per cent of all American adults were not planning to take a vacation that year, and the number was as high as 68 per cent in the Northeast.[1] At approximately the same time, however, the Hyatt Corporation had a slightly different story to tell the world. It had found a new pocket of hope, and identified the spa industry as 'one of the fastest growing trends in travel'.[2] In the years following Hyatt's announcement, the International SPA Association (ISPA) confirmed this observation with a series of larger statistical analyses, which depicted the spa industry from North America and Europe to Asia as an industry in a phase of vigorous growth.[3]

In Sweden, practitioners working in segments of the health and hotel industries were attuned to a similar trend that had been developing since the years around the millennium. Spas were not actually a new phenomenon in the world of Swedish tourism. They had a history dating back to the late seventeenth century, but in Sweden

9

the continuity of that history was broken over the course of the twentieth century when many of the country's largest and most prestigious resorts were either forced into bankruptcy, or severely hobbled by economic uncertainties as they fell out of public favor. By the early 2000s, however, that trend had more than reversed itself. Rooms were being filled at a rate that many spas had not seen in over a hundred years, and revenues were up – dramatically – increasing in some cases at an annual rate of between fifty and eighty percent.[4]

All of this sounded promising, but nonetheless, behind all of this good news one could still detect a degree of uncertainty and nervousness, as spa managers in Sweden struggled to size up their competition while simultaneously developing a better feel for the desires and expectations of their patrons. Which trends were going to prove popular? Which ones were falling off? Could they truly be certain that the spa phenomenon had arrived to stay, or would it fade as rapidly as it caught on?

Facing these questions, older spas moved quickly to distance themselves from anything that might make the general public associate them with health farms (which by the late 1990s were stigmatized as being dreadfully boring), while newer spas – often built as a complement to already existing hotel facilities – endeavored to make sense out of the wide array of alternatives they faced. Where many hotels had once tried to survive the long dark winter months of the Swedish off-season by offering dinner and dancing weekend packages, or Saturday night discos for the twenty-something crowd, they were about to redefine themselves as part of a 'wellness industry'. But what exactly did that mean? How could one culturally orchestrate the production of serenity and make people feel both relaxed and recharged at one and the same time – weren't these somewhat contradictory processes? What types of services, treatments, activities, and facilities should one invest in? And what types of magic would you have to cast to make a wound-up and stressed-out middle-aged couple feel relaxed and rejuvenated over the course of a weekend getaway, without ever making them feel bored or uncomfortable?

There were, in short, challenges to be faced, but these challenges were not limited to the echelons of spa managers and their employees. The people visiting these places had to develop and learn a whole new repertoire of cultural competencies, dispositions, and codes of conduct before they would be able to feel comfortable in the world of spas. What to wear to a mud bath? Would you be deemed inconsiderate if you were to speak to your spouse while lounging in the 'relax room', or if you made a short business call on your cell phone? It was one thing to say that you wanted to go to a spa to relax, but after you had arrived, just what were you supposed to do, when you were doing nothing?

For the anthropologist, these and similar questions were interesting points of departure for an analysis of an increasingly popular and rapidly growing segment of the tourism and leisure industry. Indeed, much of what follows will be of direct relevance for scholars, practitioners, and laymen interested in tourism and leisure generally, and spas specifically. However, one of the objectives of this book is to place the spa phenomenon in a larger cultural context than that defined in terms of tourism and leisure.

The cultural economy

Spa operators speak fervently about the production of wellness and well-being, but their work involves the selling of lifestyles, the conversion of Eastern philosophies into market-based commodities, the production of aura and atmosphere, and the management of guests' emotional states. Health and relaxation are the epitaphs used by spa managers and marketers to describe their activities and attract visitors, but much of what is actually being done in and around these facilities can be understood in terms of the packaging, staging, and commoditization of culture, affect, and experience. Spas, in other words, are arenas of economic activity that, while ever-focused on profit margins and the bottom line, are perpetually dependent upon a great deal of cultural work in order to achieve their goals. They are places in which cultural and economic processes are intimately entangled, and are in this sense part of a larger phenomenon which some scholars have described as a 'cultural economy' (du Gay & Pryke 2002).

Now, the manner and degree to which cultural and economic processes are entangled in one another is a phenomenon which has attracted increased attention and scholarly debate over the course of the last couple of decades. One of the more important works to focus on this nexus was *The Economy of Signs* by Scott Lash and John Urry (1994), in which they put forward the argument that modern society had entered a phase of development in which the distinction between cultural and economic processes had become increasingly blurred. As they argued, 'economic and symbolic processes are more than ever interlaced and interarticulated; that is, ... the economy is increasingly culturally inflected and...culture is more and more economically inflected. Thus the boundary between the two becomes more and more blurred' (Lash and Urry, 1994: 64). The argument put forward here pointed to the growing economic significance that could be attributed to the mass media, advertising, and the symbolic value of signs, but in so doing it also drew attention to the degree to which the economy was increasingly grounded in abstract cultural processes linked to the production of such things as lifestyles, cultural identities, and the aesthetics of everyday life.

Amongst the reactions provoked by *The Economy of Signs* and other theoretically related works were questions concerning the processes of blurring that Lash and Urry pointed out. Some scholars, such as Larry Ray and Andrew Sayer (1999), agreed that there was a need to understand better the manner in which cultural and economic processes were increasingly interrelated, but they took issue with the notion that the distinction between culture and economy was in the process of disappearing, or had become so weak as to be no longer of analytical significance. In reaction, they argued that if this border had ceased to be tenable, then the words it separated, 'culture' and 'economy', would in essence be synonymous. And since culture and economy were clearly not synonyms, then there must still exist an analytical need not only to keep them separated, but equally to understand the distinctions between them. Anything else, Ray and Sayer asserted, would serve to do little else than produce confusion. As they argued, 'there are still crucial differences between culture and economy, and ... it is politically as well as theoretically important to understand them' (1999: 4).

As a correction, Ray and Sayer endeavored to argue for a need to understand culture and economy as different and distinct, if nonetheless interconnected, realms of human life. Admittedly, they conceded, all economic processes and activities had to be understood at some level as 'culturally inflected or "embedded"' since they could never be 'conducted independently of systems of meanings and norms' (1999: 6). However, from their point of view, one of the primary factors which distinguish the realm of the economic from that of the cultural is the extent to which 'economic activities and processes involve a primarily instrumental orientation; they are ultimately a means to an end, satisfying external goals to do with provisioning' (ibid.), while in contrast, the values associated with culture are intrinsic and non-instrumental (1999: 5). Yet in arguing in this way, Ray and Sayer created a rather large problem for themselves, which relates to the question of context. As du Gay and Pryke point out:

> any attempt to instigate categorical distinctions between 'intrinsi-cally' and 'instrumentally' oriented activity in order to support a general normative analysis of economic and cultural life will quickly come up against brute empirical realities that it will not be able to account for or make much reasonable sense of (2002: 11).

In other words, instead of taking the distinction between culture and economy as a naturalized given, scholars should be focusing upon the daily contexts and settings they are observing, and questioning the manners in which the realms of the cultural and economic are entwined and interacting. As du Gay and Pryke pointed out (ibid.), issues of intrinsic value versus instrumental value, and the significances associated with them, have shifted in different historical and cultural contexts. In moving to fortify the boundary between culture and economy as Ray and Sayer did, one risks producing a rather static understanding of the qualities attributed to both culture and economy while simultaneously erecting a highly inflexible model of the relationship between the two. Yet clearly, this is not to say that culture and economy are one and the same thing.

Few scholars (and least of all Lash or Urry) would ever claim that words like 'culture' and 'economy' could ever be used synonymously or interchangeably. The practice of economics is built around established knowledge, discourses, practices, rationalities, and management strategies that have real consequences in the world around us, and which we can speak (and think) about in terms of economics. And this is true even if economics is always, *a priori*, culturally embedded. Culture, on the other hand, as it is generally used in discussions of the cultural economy, and as it will be invoked throughout this book, is derived from an anthropological understanding of the concept. That is to say, while it is symbolically laden and includes forms of expression commonly aligned with 'high culture' (such as music, dance, art, literature, and the like), it is broader than this. Culture is the process through which competing and often conflicting understandings and interpretations of the world around us are generated, structured, signified, and ultimately shared and contested. Culture in this sense is not a static or bounded entity, neither is it anything which a person or group of people 'has'. It is ever-shifting. As some have pointed out (see Hannerz 1992: 4; O'Dell 2002: 35 ff.) it can be likened to a river. When viewed from a distance, it may seem to be something which is permanently etched into the landscape, but as you approach the river it becomes apparent that it is ever-flowing, swirling, and changing.

In speaking of a cultural economy, or the culturalization of the economy in the context of this book, my intention is to align myself with the growing cadre of scholars who are challenging the traditional dualistic manner of viewing culture and economy as separate and distinct. As others have pointed out, entrepreneurs do not hesitate to borrow concepts once anchored in disciplines such as anthropology and sociology, freely invoking them to their own advantage as they sell products and services through appeals to culture, lifestyle, identity, aura, and authenticity (Aronsson 2007: 16 ff.; Löfgren & Willim 2005: 12). However, this is not a new phenomenon. General Motors, for example, realized in the early twentieth century that they were in the business of selling dreams, lifestyles, and identities. They consequently structured their organization to excel in these areas and came (at least for a while) to eclipse their competitors who, in contrast, tended to view cars more as machines than fashion (Gartman 1994). And while management gurus tried to rethink their field in the 1980s by arguing for the need to understand 'corporate culture' (Deal & Kennedy 2000), by the turn of the century they had moved on to write books and articles focusing on *Funky Business* (Ridderstråle & Nordström 2002), *Serious Play* (Schrage 1999), *Storytelling* (Mossberg & Nissen Johansen 2006), *The Rise of the Creative Class* (Florida 2002), *The Pursuit of Wow!* (Peters 1994), *My Voodoo* (Firth & Carayol 2002), and 'Magic in Action' (Berg 2003).

At the same time, anthropologists, sociologists, and other social scientists were increasingly turning their attention to the realms of business, work, and economy, examining arenas of activity ranging from advertising (McFall 2002), IT companies (Willim 2002), the performative strategies of middle-level corporate managers (Thrift 2000a), and the introduction of New Age philosophies to management theory (Heelas 2002; Goldschmidt Salamon 2005), to the packaging of events (Ristilammi 2002), experiences (Christersdotter 2005; O'Dell 2005a), feelings (Thrift 2004), passions (Amin & Thrift 2007), and aesthetics in business contexts (Pine & Gilmore 1999). In short, a growing body of work has been developing which helps explain the many ways in which culture and economy are entwined in one another.

Nonetheless, there are a few problems with this work that should be addressed. To begin with, while others have pointed out that there is still an all-too-strong temptation to view the cultural economy as a new epoch in economic (and perhaps cultural) history (du Gay & Pryke 2002: 7; O'Dell 2002; Ray & Sayer 1999: 7), very little work has actually endeavored to correct this bias. There is a need here to open the field of cultural economics to a historical perspective that links into the present, and provides more depth to our understanding of the ways in which cultural and economic processes have been entangled over time and in varying contexts.

Beyond this, there has been too great a tendency, particularly in the social sciences, to skew the focus of analysis to spheres of activity linked to white-collar jobs and the creative industries. Consequently, one could develop the mistaken impression that the entanglement of culture and economic processes is a phenomenon primarily affecting specific (dare we call them cultured?) segments of the population in Western society. It is time to reflect more seriously upon the manner in which these processes are also embedded in low- and modest-paying sectors of the service economy, and find expression in spheres of daily life not limited to the workplace.

It could be argued that portions of the work in tourism studies have done just this, but the tendency in much of this work has been to define tourism and the practices associated with tourism in contrast to everyday life, rather than as an integrated aspect of it. Here, the insistence with which tourism scholars have defined their subject of study in terms of liminality, or as distinctively different from leisure activities in general, has hampered their ability to argue convincingly that the processes they are describing might be integrated aspects of daily life in general.[5] There is, I would argue, an urgent need here to jettison the concept of liminality, and more stringently investigate the ways in which the services and practices associated with tourism and leisure are integrated with everyday life.

The rise of the ephemeral

This has been one of the primary impetuses for the project at hand, which developed out of previous work I conducted on segments of the service sector associated with tourism and the experience economy.[6] The objective of this earlier work was to develop new theoretical and analytical understandings of the ways in which experiences were produced, staged, and consumed in modern society. However, one of the major theoretical inspirations for this work was itself a reaction to the overwhelming attention that Joseph Pine and James Gilmore received in Scandinavia in connection with the publication of their book, *The Experience Economy* (1999).

The central message of the book was concise and easy to understand. 'Experiences represent an existing but previously unarticulated *genre of economic output*. Decoupling experiences from services in accounting for what businesses create opens up possibilities for extraordinary economic expansion.' (1999: ix ff.) The realm of experience was in other words an underdeveloped arena, and potential source of rapid and dynamic economic expansion. It was, Pine and Gilmore argued, the next stage of economic development that modern societies were about to enter. Following a line of argumentation which rested upon a simplified unilinear model of economic evolution in which society seemingly moved through a series of very distinct stages (from commodity exchange, to goods production, to service offerings), Pine and Gilmore argued that Western society was now in the process of making the next leap; this time into the experience economy.[7]

In Scandinavia, this line acquired the resonance of a political and economic manifesto as politicians, actors in the tourist industry, academics, and other public servants all saw what they perceived to be an untapped well of potential economic growth and employment opportunities. While tourism prospered and expanded rapidly in other parts of the world, the Scandinavian countries, with their short summers and relatively high prices, had found it difficult to cash in on this market. Pine and Gilmore essentially offered an alternative to the old cornerstones of tourism: sun, sand, and sin. Experiences could be produced and sold anywhere. They were not confined to beachfront properties or dependent upon specific weather conditions – or so the logic of the times seemed to dictate.

However, the Scandinavian countries were not alone in their interest in the realm of experiences. On the contrary, *The Experience Economy* was full of American and European examples, ranging from amusement parks and themed restaurants to supermarkets in suburban neighborhoods, all already striving to produce and stage experiences. The attempt to commodify experience was, in short, already big business globally (and remains so to this day). Nonetheless, the primary factor which distinguished the Scandinavian interest in the realm of experiences from events already underway in North America and other parts of the world was the degree to which the concept of the experience economy was put on the political agenda, and became something which politicians, tourism, city planners, and municipal leaders actively endeavored to develop and implement.

Consequently, *The Experience Economy* became not only a political manifesto, but also a handbook for economic reform and societal change. Cities and regions were branded in an attempt to provide them with new, 'hot' identities. Local cultures were catalogued and mapped in order to identify what it was that made them unique, and thereby marketable. Funds were pumped into peripheral rural villages in the hope that they would develop into vibrant meeting-grounds for academics, municipal authorities, and private experience-oriented businesses.[8] And attempts were made to push groups of citizens who were deemed to be undesirable (such as youths and immigrants) out of the centers of cities such as Copenhagen so that these urban environments might better meet the expectations of a coherent 'national culture' that tourists associated them with.

In this context, the discussions that *The Experience Economy* generated were of a highly instrumental nature. How could you best facilitate economic growth by investing in the realm of experiences? How could one create new creative environments and meeting-places that could contribute to this growth and continuously renew it? Numerically, how large did a population have to be to support the development of new theme parks? Very few of the actors propagating for the need to invest in the realm of experiences stopped to ask why people seemed to be searching for new experiences. More importantly, even fewer people, inside or outside of academia, seemed to be interested in the consequences all of this could have culturally. Where Pine and Gilmore had laid out a recipe for economic expansion and larger profit margins, there was a need to consider analytically the broader effects the interest in the realm of experiences had in practice.

The issues I raise here could (and should) be addressed in any of a number of empirical fields. The choice to study spas was in part a question of timing. The spa industry was entering a period of rapid expansion in the early years of the new millennium, at the same time that I was developing an interest in the types of questions noted here, and public discussions about the experience economy were becoming increasingly prevalent in Sweden. Yet as an object of study, spas were interesting because they did have a history, and in the case of the Swedish spas, it was a history which stretched back to the late seventeenth century. As such, they were well suited for a study of the cultural economy that did more than focus upon the present. Here it was possible to use the past as a foil against which one could view the present, and indeed this is the object of the following chapter. Today, spas present themselves in a manner that is easy to take for granted: as sites of inner and outer healing and individual pampering, at which guests can get away from the stresses of daily life and

Futons, hammocks, an abundance of cushions, and close proximity to the heavens and nature were all important components in spas' attempt to provide their patrons with a sense of well-being. Photo: Tom O'Dell.

get in touch with themselves. As the following chapter illustrates, spas have not always framed their services in this way. The manner in which they organize and define their services today is unique – a reflection on the times in which we live – but an appreciation of this fact would be impossible to obtain without first establishing a clearer historically anchored understanding of how a Swedish spa was organized previously. In this way, the following chapter offers a contrast to the world of spas today, revealing in the process some of the various ways in which the cultural economy could work in the eighteenth and nineteenth centuries.

Yet spas are also interesting sites at which to study the cultural economy and the production of experiences, because they are so explicitly focused upon the manipulation of the body and senses through the material world. The products they strive to offer (serenity, harmony, balance, and so on) are highly ephemeral, but what spas actually do is very concrete and physical. This is a world in which the material culture of spas matters (Miller 1998b), because it is one of the primary avenues through which spas endeavor to have an affect upon their guests – from terry cloth robes and towels to massage tables and special oils. Materiality and corporeality are inseparable here, but they are also bound to the limited space of the spa facility itself, and can be studied in relation to it. And thus, while experiences and the entanglement of culture and economy in one another may be highly ephemeral subjects of study, spas are apposite places in which to study them – if nothing else, because they are limited spaces that are designed and intended to be affective.

The spas

The material on which this book rests comes from a number of diverse sources. The following chapter, which discusses eighteenth- and nineteenth-century Swedish spas and the activities that took place there, is based on historical materials obtained from Lund University Library and the Regional State Archive in Lund. In addition, a smaller amount of material has been gathered from the Internet, in part composed of contemporary promotional materials used by spas today, as well as statistics, reports, and journalistic accounts produced by actors involved in the spa industry. But in part this material includes older texts and documents dating back to the nineteenth century that have been scanned and digitalized. Other contemporary materials such as magazines, newspaper articles, and brochures have also been used. Over the past few years I have spent a considerable amount of time scanning the shelves of local newspaper stands for articles about spas. At first this only provided intermittent rewards in the form of the occasional travel magazine feature. Over the years, however, spas have begun to appear on a regular basis in all sorts of magazines, ranging from interior design magazines to health, travel, and women's magazines. Due to the volume of material currently being produced in the mass media that is related to spas, I have had to be selective, and tended to purchase only those Swedish magazines featuring longer articles on spas, regardless of the genre of the magazine.

Larger sections of the book, however, are based upon interviews I conducted with spa guests, personnel, and managers, and my own observations on spas. It should be noted that I am not an avid spa-goer. On the contrary, I had never been to a spa before I began conducting the research for this book, and had at best only a very vague notion of what a spa was, or what life at a spa entailed. Through a contact I made after an open lecture I gave at Lund University, I was extended an invitation to spend a few days at Varbergs Kurort on the Swedish west coast, south of Gothenburg (Göteborg), where I would be the guest of the facility's manager. The visit was intended as a first inquiry into the world of spas. Over the course of my stay I interviewed members of the management team as well as personnel working in the spa, received a full tour of the facility, and experienced my first spa treatments (which were chosen for me by the spa manager): a seaweed massage, and an aloe vera wrap. This was a world strikingly different from anything to which I was accustomed.

An initial review of the literature on spas and repeated searches of the Internet revealed that this was not a unitary world. Going to a spa in Sweden was different from going to a spa in Eastern Europe, where the medical traditions associated with spas still have a vibrant life. France and Germany had their own traditions, also closer to the medical heritage of hydrotherapy than that presently found in Sweden, but nonetheless inflected with national characteristics of their own. And countries such as Thailand were dead set on reinvigorating older Asian traditions to meet the demands of the modern market.[9]

Until that point I had been considering a cross-cultural comparison as a means of gaining a perspective on the Swedish context. However, its implementation would pose the question of why prefer one

Sunchairs and towels were part of the basic material culture that spas relied upon as they strove to work magic and mass-produce serenity. Photo: Tom O'Dell.

particular comparison, or set of comparisons, over another. Granted, there were similarities between settings. This was, after all, a growing global market, and there were recipes to follow. Indeed, while the material upon which this book is based was drawn from the Swedish context, it has been invoked with the intention of illuminating trends that are pervasive and rapidly expanding throughout the global spa market. Nonetheless, it must be acknowledged that there are differences between national settings that have historical explanations of their own, and it was against this background that I decided to focus my study upon the Swedish context, and use Sweden's own history as a means of gaining a perspective on the phenomena taking place in spas at present. Working in this way, my intention here has been to use the Swedish context as a means of analytically and theoretically gaining an insight into the manner in which the cultural economy can (and does) work not only in Sweden, but also far beyond its borders.

Before proceeding, however, the focus of the study had to be sharpened a notch further. As it turns out, the difference between particular types of spas was occasionally larger than could be explained in terms of national or cultural distinction. There were day spas, destination spas, medical spas, hotel spas, and many others – and each type of spa was unique. Medical spas could offer forms of surgery and body modification, while day spas usually offered massages, shorter treatments, and cosmetic consultation, and hotel spas offered larger packages in which guests could stay for a single night or several weeks, receiving not only accommodation, but even meals, treatments, diverse recreational activities, and even personal counseling in some cases.

Based upon my interest in the staging, production, and consumption of experiences, I opted to focus upon larger hotel spas. In part this was due to the fact that these were the spas (at least some of them) which had histories of their own that I wanted to draw into the analysis, but equally I realized that if one of my goals was to observe what people were actually doing in spas, and addressing the question of how experiences came to form, I needed to work in an environment in which I could melt into the background and observe from a distance. Day spas and medical spas were not appropriate here. Medical spas were an almost non-existent segment of the Swedish spa world when I began my study in the early 2000s, and they were not necessarily focused upon experience production, but instead on the delivery of physical modification services. Day spas were for the most part too small to work in as a participant observer, since many of them were organized around waiting-rooms and treatment rooms. The larger hotel spas allowed me the opportunity to move between pool, jacuzzi, restaurant, treatment rooms, and hotel facilities. They served larger numbers of guests every day (in some cases hundreds of guests circulated over the course of the day) than day spas did, and this made it possible for me to observe without disturbing them. In practice this meant that I was quite often watching what people were doing without them being aware of it.

This raises ethical issues concerning complicity and integrity, but to some extent this is a necessary move that has long been used in the social sciences and humanities as part of the effort to analyze the micro-processes of daily life (Goffman 1971; Hall 1990; Löfgren & Ehn 2007; Moran 2007). In order to address the ethical issues,

I have endeavored to keep the analysis of people's practices in the spa at a highly abstracted level, focusing upon particular practices rather than the individuals engaging in them. Indeed, throughout the book I have striven to maintain the anonymity of the people with whom I spoke: all their names have been changed; and when citing interviews with personnel, or people in managerial positions at particular spas, I have tried to maintain their anonymity by referring only vaguely to their exact positions, and if possible by not even referring to the particular spa at which they were employed.

Similar principles proved to be difficult to maintain when it came to the actual places in which I conducted observations and interviewed personnel. As it turned out, observations I made in four specific spas dominate the empirical material which is analyzed in chapters three and four, even if observations were conducted in a number of other facilities not directly discussed here. Wherever possible, I have tried not to mention facilities by their real names. In practice, however, anonymity proved to be impossible. Many of the spas I describe here have unique profiles, as do most of the larger Swedish spas which I could have chosen to work in. Anyone remotely interested in Swedish spas will undoubtedly recognize the facilities whose material culture and profile I describe in depth in chapters three and four, even if I had changed the names of these facilities. Similar problems would have arisen independent of the question of which facilities I chose to focus upon. Beyond this, the analysis also draws upon published promotional materials, and the references cited here point directly to the spas in question. Rather than attempting to thinly veil the names of the primary facilities under analysis in these chapters, I have opted to accept the fact that the facilities I am describing are identifiable. This has quite simply been inevitable. Consequently, I use their real names, while altering the names of secondary facilities that informants mention.

Choosing to work in this way, however, necessitates a particular sensitivity to the manner in which empirical materials are presented. Information which may be sensitive concerning such things as profit margins, growth rates, or particular personnel troubles are brought into the analysis in a general manner that does not directly link them to any particular facility. Some readers may wish that I had been more specific and associated some of these types of materials to named spas, but here I have intentionally worked to avoid this. I am attempting to point out trends, problems, and possibilities amongst a particular segment of spas and spa-goers in order to understand the cultural dynamics of the phenomenon at hand, not to soil or enhance the reputation of any facility or its clientele.

The organization of the book

The book is divided into four chapters. Each chapter has been written so that it can be read individually, although there are several themes that run throughout the book. The first theme I take up concerns the notion of hospitality. Having chosen to focus upon spa hotels, I found myself conducting research on an industry (the hotel industry) which defined itself in terms of hospitality. The question was: what did this mean in the world of spas? Spas do not merely offer room and board, but also wellness and better health. This at least is their claim. And in a sense, this makes spas the ultimate hospitable space – one that not only protects and nourishes the strangers it takes in under its roof, but even promises to make them feel better when they leave than when they arrived. But there is a catch: it is a conditional form of hospitality that is market-driven, and not open to all. In this sense, one might argue, this is not hospitality at all.

Chapter two traces the notion of hospitality back in history and problematizes the concept itself. It endeavors to demonstrate how the managers of spas worked in the eighteenth and nineteenth centuries to create hospitable spaces for their guests and surrounding members of the community. Evidently, spas in the eighteenth and nineteenth centuries functioned and were organized in a slightly different way from now – relying on the activities of both priests and doctors to care for the inner and outer well-being of their guests. While the chapter focuses upon the notion of hospitality and the production of hospitable spaces in the past, one objective of the chapter is also to present an ethnographic cross-section of how spa life took shape in the past, to demonstrate that while Swedish spas do have a history that bears with it certain continuities, there are also differences at work here.

Chapter three moves the discussion into the present and takes a closer look at what spas say they can provide their guests and how they do it. As the chapter points out, where spas once employed priests to care for their guests' spiritual well-being, spas today work in new ways to care for their guests, inside and out. Protestant priests can no longer be found working at Swedish spas, but the significance of the spiritual dimension has not been lost. New Age philosophies are now a highly prevalent, and an expected, aspect of a spa visit in Sweden as well as throughout much of the global spa market. In order to understand this, the chapter examines the concept of magic as it has been used previously in anthropology, and reflects upon the significance this concept might have as a phenomenon still at work in modern society.

While chapter three discusses the manner in which magic might be understood to be at work in modern spas, chapter four brings the body and senses more fully into the picture. It examines the manner in which the experiences of well-being, luxury, and pampering are created in combination with the material culture of the spa, and it addresses the question of how emotions are produced, formed, and affected via market-driven forces. Here the experiences of guests are juxtaposed with the experiences and practices of spa employees (the magicians in charge of the processes of rejuvenation that spas unleash). The question is, what type of a hospitable space is the spa today, and on whose terms?

The final chapter brings the spa home. It seeks to problematize the manner in which the cultural economy has facilitated the development of a new structure of attention increasingly focused upon working our emotions. As the chapter argues, the processes taking place in spas are not unique to them, but are spreading more widely through society. Here it is the history of the bathroom and bathroom practices that are the focus of the analysis.

CHAPTER 2

Spas and the Shifting Context of Conditional Hospitality

In July 1899 the guests at Ramlösa Brunn, a spa located on the southwestern coast of Sweden, were presented with the opportunity to purchase that year's edition of the spa newspaper, *Ramlösa-Hallået*. The newspaper included short articles, poems, stories, jokes, and puns written by the resort's visitors. These small texts were in turn framed by a wealth of advertisements placed along the outer edges of each of the newspaper's pages, promoting the products and services offered by the local merchants and professionals: from velocipedes, jewelry, and parasols to eyeglasses, men's clothing, and legal services. Proceeds earned from the newspaper were earmarked for 'the poor and sickly at Ramlösa Brunn as well as the retirement fund for the bathing assistants' at the resort (1899: 1).

Featured on the front page of the paper was a poem, 'Compassion', whose tone endeavored to remind readers that while many of those at Ramlösa Brunn were well-off and enjoyed a good life, such was not the case for everyone. The poem ended with the following lines:

> But do not hand out that of mere, hard metal
> A few paltry, quickly spent pieces
> And do not let your hand be hard and cold
> Nor let your eyes lack the adornment of feeling
>
> For this other is your brother, remember this,
> Who perhaps by mere chance was born a problem child
> And it has been said that out of compassion
> A brother once bled on the cross for us. (Thornberg 1899: 1)

And finally, next to this poem, the reader found the love story of a young sickly woman named Aina, and the chance encounter she had with an unnamed male suitor at Ramlösa Brunn. It was a story of walks through the park, infatuation, the sweet smell of flowers, confessions of love, and ultimately, the heartbreaking disappointment of winter, distance, and broken promises.

Ramlösa-Hallået was perhaps not so much a newspaper as a short, entertaining distraction available to guests at the resort. However, when viewed from today's perspective, it constitutes an interesting time capsule that hints at the contours of an arena of health, hospitality, and leisure which was rather different from the world of Swedish spas that exists today. Look again at *Ramlösa-Hallået* and we begin to see the opening of a space of hospitality that combines elements of a modern capitalist and commercial economy with older, more traditional patriarchal and religious moralities. It is a space in which very different categories of people move about (from Sweden's economic elite to the down-trodden, all of whom are cared for by servants without secure pension benefits). And it is a space to which some came to be healed, some came to relax and enjoy themselves, and some came for both purposes.

In contemporary society, and particularly by industry analysts, spas are generally regarded as an integrated aspect of the hospitality industry, but little attention has been devoted to an analysis of what this really means. As a means of exploring this question, this chapter begins by revisiting the concept of hospitality, first from a philosophical perspective, and then by placing it in a historic context. The source material from the nineteenth and early twentieth centuries is then used to discuss the manner in which an increasingly commercialized atmosphere of hospitality came to be culturally organized to accommodate a clientele that became ever more diverse. In closing, the chapter argues for a need to more stringently interrogate the conditions under which spaces of hospitality operate, and through which they affect those under their auspices.

Hospitality: rights and obligations

Does hospitality consist in interrogating the new arrival? Does it begin with the question addressed to the newcomer (which seems very human and sometimes loving, assuming that hospitality should be linked to love …): what is your name? … Or else does hospitality begin with the unquestioning welcome, in a double effacement, the effacement of the question *and* the name? Is it more just and more loving to question or not to question? to call by the name or without the name? (Derrida 2000: 27–29)

So, what is hospitality? On one level, hospitality is a phenomenon readily aligned with notions of the home and private spheres of daily life. It implies the opening of our homes to guests and strangers, and the taking of a solicitous stance as we extend shelter, sustenance, and entertainment to those guests. The offering of hospitality in this context is an act or practice that many would associate with feelings of warmth, openness, and friendliness.

On another level, however, hospitality is also a phenomenon that is very strongly aligned with the world beyond the private confines of the home. A simple search on the Internet provides a staggering ninety-two million hits after a search time of seven hundredths of a second. But here references to the home are few and far between.[1] Instead, if we are to believe the search engines of the Internet, hospitality turns out to be something that could be understood in terms of such key-words as 'jobs', 'services', 'consultants', 'design', 'franchises', 'human resources', 'investment', 'lodging', 'sales and marketing', 'supplies and equipment', and 'travel'.[2] Rather than being associated with the private relations between hosts and guests, hospitality in this context is more impersonal, a reified commodity whose qualities can be managed, optimized, and measured, and whose accessibility can be steered toward particular market segments and demographic groups (Bowen & Ford 2004; Testa & Sipe 2006). The sheer volume of information related to market-bound forms of hospitality attests to the degree to which hospitality has come to be understood as both an industry and industrial product/service.

Against this background, it is perhaps not surprising to find that it currently seems so 'natural' to speak of hospitality in terms of services provided, or travel and lodging opportunities. But the movement of hospitality into the market, and particularly its organization into an 'industry', is a development predominantly anchored in the twentieth century – although as the proceeding chapter illustrates, this is a phenomenon with roots stretching further back than this (Woods 1991). Indeed, the formation of something that we today unreflectingly refer to as the hospitality industry is itself intimately linked to the development of university-based management programs that developed after the Second World War under the mantle of 'hospitality management'. To be sure, the world of hotels and restaurants has a long history of its own, but the transformation of hospitality into an industry is a process that is intricately entwined with the development of university-bound institutions of hospitality management, and their endeavors to delineate a new field of study and hands-on managerial practices that would facilitate the expansion and economic profitability of establishments primarily located in the world of restaurants and hotels, as well as segments of neighboring branches such as entertainment and tourism (Airey & Tribe 2000). 'Hospitality' worked well as a vaguely defined catch-all concept under which academics could gather their activities, organize themselves, and argue for the institutionalization of a new discipline of study – an argument which was believed to have been strengthened by the sheer numbers of people one could say were employed by this 'industry', and the amount of revenue it generated (and the more that was included under the umbrella of 'hospitality', the more substantial these numbers seemed to become).

The question is what the establishment of this way of thinking about and framing hospitality has done to our means of understanding it. For example, if hospitality is understood on one level to be bound to the relationship between guests and hosts, then what does it mean to 'manage hospitality'? How can a social relationship be 'franchised', 'rationalized', or made 'more effective', to use just a few of the tropes in vogue in the hospitality management literature? These are all words and associations that are largely taken for granted today in relation to commercialized forms of hospitality. However, to the extent that this is true, it can be argued that scholars in the field of hospitality management have been more active in creating new buzzwords and models of hospitality than in reflecting upon the meaning of the concept itself. As a consequence, very little attention has been devoted to a closer examination of the cultural context in which commercialized forms of hospitality operate, and out of which they are generated. And even less attention has been paid to the question of what the commercialization of hospitality has done to popular understandings of its limits and contents, as well as the shifting expectations people invest in it.

Hospitality, as it turns out, is not just a service or product that certain institutions have tried to package and sell. It is simultaneously a politically and ethically laden activity (Germann Molz & Gibson 2007). As Couze Venn has pointed out, drawing upon Derrida, 'hospitality inherently calls up the ethical since it implicates the welcoming of the other, the stranger, or the neighbor' (2002: 73). In the process, it begs such questions as to whom is our hospitality open, to whom do we open it, and under what circumstances? As it turns out, there is much more at issue here than the friendly and solicitous behavior of a benevolent host in the confines of her/his home, or the selling of a service on the open market.

The roots of the word hospitality are found in the Latin *hostis*, etymologically linked to such modern English words as 'guest', 'stranger', and 'enemy' (Derrida 2000: 45; Dikeç 2002: 229) as well as 'host', 'hospice', and 'hospital' (Sandoval-Strausz 2007: 138; *Webster's New World Dictionary* 1986: 678).[3] At the same time, it receives much of its cultural energy through its propensity to arouse associations that link it to the home and the implicit borders of the home (Derrida 2000; Venn 2002: 73). In this sense, hospitality implies the coming and entrance of the guest, the unlocking of the front door, the opening of one's kitchen, the circulation of goods and foods, the offering of a space before the hearth or in the parlor, and ultimately, a point of departure at which the guest bids adieu and moves on. To speak of hospitality is thus not only to speak of a relationship implicating guests and hosts, but, just as importantly, to speak of the making of space and the cultural orchestration of border crossings and mobility.

However, opening one's home to guests or strangers is a potentially dangerous endeavor – a gesture which can be abused. It is an act which potentially obligates the guest to submit to certain rules of engagement; rules which Derrida has referred to as the 'laws of hospitality' (Derrida 2000: 75 ff.), which place conditions upon the types of behaviors and actions that fall within the realm of acceptability. And while both the host and her/his guests must follow the laws of hospitality, this is nonetheless an asymmetrical relationship in which the host presumes, or is presumed, to rule. Thus, while welcoming and entertaining guests, we close certain doors in our homes to them, and construct symbolic boundaries which they are expected to respect and not cross, and in this sense 'we seek to honor our guests and at the same time keep them at a distance' (Featherstone 2002: 6). But is it really possible to speak of hospitality, in a context of mastery, domination, and asymmetrical relations – a context that depends on the laying out of the law?

Bearing this question in mind, Derrida distinguishes between 'absolute hospitality' and 'conditional hospitality' (Derrida 2000: 25 ff.).

> Absolute hospitality requires that I open up my home and that I give not only to the foreigner ... but to the absolute, unknown, anonymous other, and that I *give place* to them, that I let them come, that I let them arrive, and take place in the place I offer them, without asking of them either reciprocity (entering into a pact) or even their names. (Derrida 2000: 25)

Absolute hospitality is pure hospitality without constraint, a giving without obligation, without debt; it is thus different from a gift in the Maussian sense (Mauss 1990). It implies the unconditional welcoming of the complete stranger, whom Derrida wonders if it is possible to welcome without even asking her/his name. No questions, no demands or expectations of reciprocity, just openness – and hospitality. Conditional hospitality, on the other hand, is what most of us are accustomed to. It is hospitality with rules and expectations, in which guests understand that there are limits to the types of behavior that their host will tolerate.

In practice, absolute hospitality may be all but impossible, but as a concept it destabilizes all conventions that might be taken for granted as given aspects of (conditional) hospitality. In the discrepancy that arises out of the tension between absolute and conditional hospitality, we more clearly see the significance played by openings, in addition to processes of recognition (Dikeç 2002: 229). For the host, this implies not only the opening of the *domus* to the world, but even a preparedness to open oneself to that which is not of the home – that which is somewhat foreign, different, and strange. This is an opening that is impossible without at least a modicum of recognition of the needs, wants, and desires of the guest (the other) – a process that is itself dependent upon some form of recognition of the life circumstances of the other, or at least a willingness to listen and learn of those circumstances. After all, how could one possibly be hospitable without some form of understanding or willingness to listen?

However, these openings and processes of recognition are not limited to the host, for guests must also assume a similar stance as they enter the home territory of another – and enter a world in which not even the most trivial routines are performed in the same way as they are at home. To accept the hospitality of the host is to accept not only the host's benevolence, but also her/his difference. The question, as one moves from a position of absolute hospitality to one of conditional hospitality, becomes where to draw the boundaries of openness and recognition. In what ways are both the guest and the host prepared to expose themselves to the openings of the other, and to recognize the circumstances out of which these openings are made? And in a world of conditions, how are spaces of hospitality culturally organized, to the extent they can be?

Private spaces and ulterior motives

Bearing these questions in mind, it should be acknowledged that writing about hospitality in relation to spas positions the subject in a rather special context that is worth reflecting upon.[4] In many ways, it might be argued that the offering and extension of hospitality was, from the very beginning, a phenomenon centrally concerned not only with forms of provisioning, but also with issues of both health and mobility. Prior to the spread and institutionalization of commercial forms of accommodation, travel was a precarious and at times dangerous activity. The extension of private forms of hospitality that included sustenance and safe shelter was all but a prerequisite for its conduct (King 1995: 221 ff.). But to the extent that this is true, the laws of hospitality have long been limited, controlled, debated, and even subjected to political and personal interest.

In early modern England (1400–1700), for example, hospitality was perceived to be a Christian duty regulated by values and norms of behavior dating back to classical Rome. However, the exact implications of what the duties of hospitality included were contested (Heal 1990; Selwyn 2000: 21). For example, it was generally agreed that the good host had an obligation to extend his/her hospitality to the poor. Likewise, the landed elite were expected to open their households to foreigners and strangers, but the norms of the day also urged temperance and moderation. The needy (whether a neighbor or a stranger), some argued, should be cared for, but not overindulged. Unfortunately, establishing the status of a stranger was not always an easy task. Thus, while some moralists argued for the merits of restraint, others pointed to the biblical lesson of Lot, and reminded their contemporaries of the fact that even unassuming strangers could be angels in disguise, worthy of care and hospitality (Heal 1984).

Complicating matters even more, however, some critics of the time lamented what they perceived to be the decline of English hospitality (Walton 2000: 58), and the fact that in reality when hospitality was extended to the poor, it all too often implied little more than the doling out of table scraps and leftovers to those who were banished to the gatehouse (Heal 1984: 75 ff.). Instead of taking the form of an unselfish Christian duty, hospitality, it was pointed out, was increasingly directed towards peers and people of standing, taking forms that were often intended to endow the host with increased social status, honor, and political influence. In the eyes of some moralists, this raised more than a few uncomfortable questions as to whether or not this manner of giving for gain was an appropriate Christian activity (Heal 1990).

Private hospitality, in other words, was an important means of offering help, care, and provisions to strangers as well as disenfranchised members of the local community; however, it could also be used strategically to further a host's own ulterior social, political and economic objectives – and in this sense possessed qualities that many associate with commercialized forms of hospitality today (see Telfer 2000: 40 ff.). It was, in short, a morally laden social field of exchange and interaction whose bounds and limits were continuously contested and debated.

Hospital -ity

Over the course of the eighteenth and nineteenth centuries, commercial forms of hospitality came increasingly to replace many of the functions that were once tied to private hospitality. But this was a slow process in which it is possible to discern the parallel existence of older morals and norms alongside newer, more modern market-driven concerns. These processes came to particular expression in a wide range of European spa settings that united new forms of commercial leisure and secularized notions of the power of medicine (and science) with a series of older moralities and beliefs (Bacon 1997; Mackaman 1998).

In Sweden, the very first spas were established in the last decades of the seventeenth century. Their popularity amongst the Swedish royalty, aristocracy, and cultural elite played a central role in facilitating the spread and development of new facilities in the eighteenth century, at the same time as they reinforced the reputations of those which already existed (Mansén 2001). But their growth in popularity was also derived from the eclectic mix of activities that took place within and around their perimeters.

Initially, Swedish spas were established by medical doctors and practitioners who, inspired by the work being conducted by their European peers, believed that water contained hidden properties that could be revealed through careful study, and put to use in healing a wide array of diseases and ailments. The medical ambition of uncovering and harnessing the curative power of water was significant, if for no other reason than that it provided a spa visit with a particular structure, duration, and form of cultural legitimacy that would remain in place for more than two hundred years, and which centered around taking the waters as well as the medicinal application of various forms of muds, baths, and showers. The hospitality of spas could, when viewed from this perspective, be understood in terms of an ambition to not only house and feed guests, but also to closely monitor their well-being and to care for them. In order to achieve this, the hospitality of the spa was organized around a series of movements and activities which were quickly ritualized and made part of the expected rhythm of a cure. These included visits to the resort's doctor, daily trips to the resort's well to consume prescribed quantities of water, schedules of bathing, minute instructions on diet, the labor of bathing maids, and controlled exposure to fresh air.

In order to succeed in producing this amalgamation of health and hospitality, spas of the eighteenth and nineteenth century were in this sense dependent upon the degree to which they functioned as spaces of empirical inquiry in which no detail was too small for scrutiny and consideration. As part of this, everything from the waters and muds of spas to the bodies of guests were broken down into their smallest components and carefully analyzed. By 1827, for example, experts had determined that 1,000 parts of water at Ronneby Brunn, located in southeastern Sweden, contained the chemical equivalent of:

1.0686 parts	sulphate of ferrous oxide
0.0133	sulphate of zinc oxide
0.0260	sulphate of manganous oxide
0.3705	sulphate of chalky soil
0.1716	sulphate of talcum soil
0.2126	ammonia alum
0.4790	sodium alum
0.0433	potassium alum
0.0230	aluminum chloride
0.1151	silicon soil
2.5236	total[5]

For the layman, the significance of these numbers was undoubtedly more mystifying than enlightening, but when the supervisor of the spa, Doctor Hellman, published a handbook for guests which provided them with both information about the spa, and instructions on how to best prepare for their visit as well as behave while there, he nonetheless felt obligated to include four entire chapters discussing and presenting these and similar measurements. In the nineteenth-century world of spas this was a fairly common phenomenon, and similar practices could be found throughout Sweden as well as the rest of Europe (see, for example, Levertin 1990; Lindblad 1907: 20).

By distinguishing the unique properties of the water at each spa, the hope was that medical experts could then better identify the curative capacities of the waters they presided over – and use it all the more effectively to both cure their guests and market their facilities. Ultimately, this proved to be more easily handled in theory than praxis. Medical practitioners consistently failed to find definitive links between what they believed the waters at their facilities could achieve, and what they actually did.[6] As Hellman admitted:

> Since it is still not possible – even at the old European mineral wells to which the most celebrated of scholarly names are tied – to determine with certainty which ailments water can, without exception, affect specifically, it would be more than presumptuous of this author to believe that he could be able to determine, after such a short time, who could and should drink the water from Ronneby's health-well. (1860: 34)

The inability to pinpoint the specific disorders that the water at Ronneby could alleviate did not dishearten Hellman or his peers, however. On the contrary, this was usually simply interpreted as further evidence of the need to investigate the phenomenon more stringently (see Weisz 2001), because while doctors of the period may have lacked any definitive evidence, many would have echoed Hellman's observation that they, like he, 'had seen the most wonderful and surprising effects of [the water], when it has been used in the right way' (Hellman 1860: 34).

And thus, with the ambition of uncovering a few of the secrets of the healing potential of water still weighing heavily upon his shoulders, Hellman instructed patrons to bring written journals with them from their doctors, outlining their physical condition, ailments, and medications (1860: 81). As the hospitality of the spa was professionalized, and as the competition for paying patrons hardened, doctors increasingly felt pressured to explicate the manner in which their facilities could take care of those who spent time under their auspices. This implied not only opening one's doors to strangers, and extending shelter, care, and sustenance to them, but also of placing increased demands upon them. In part, these were the demands of opening one's self to the doctor's gaze, but more than this, these were also the demands of identifying oneself (and one's needs) with documents that linked patrons to a larger social network of hospitable spaces of medical care and provisioning. Conditional hospitality, as will become increasingly clear below, implied not only that the host meet the needs and desires of guests, but just as importantly that the guests themselves submit to the rules established by hosts, and indeed increasingly come prepared to help their hosts. The more doctors such as Hellman knew about the patron before them, the better were their chances of alleviating that individual's affliction, or so it was believed.

And Hellman worked hard to assure his reader that this was a place in which cures worked, presenting dozens of cases of patients and their cures. Included here was the case of a man suffering from the paralysis of the right side of his body (perhaps from a stroke) who was instructed to begin his cure by drinking a glass of water on his first day, increasing the dose by one glass a day until he was consuming five glasses per day. After the fourth day he was prescribed a mud bath followed by a rinsing in mineral water. 'On the seventh day, bitter water had to be used' (ibid.: 38). By the twenty-seventh day, after increasing doses of mineral water, the man is said to be able to stand on the bad leg, and finally he is able to walk 'relatively freely' by the thirty-sixth day. After a few years he is deemed to be completely healthy again.

In another place, Hellman described how a twenty-two-year-old woman with weak nerves began her cure by ingesting three-and-a-half mugs of water, being instructed to increase the dose gradually to five or six mugs. In addition to this she is administered a 'steel-bath' (a five-minute bath in iron-rich water) at thirty-five degrees Celsius every third day. Attesting to the beneficial effects of such measured and precise actions, it is noted that the young woman is cured of her ailment by the end of her six-week stay at the spa (ibid.: 42 ff.).

All in all, Hellman outlined the beneficial effects the waters of the spa had upon visitors suffering from such diverse illnesses as rheumatism, epilepsy, psychological disorders, hypochondria, hysteria, gastric disorders, spasms, gonorrhea, bronchitis, worms, and cardiovascular problems. In the process, and under the guise of medical motives, Hellman and his peers – both in Sweden and abroad (Bergmark 1985; Löfgren 1999; Mackaman 1998) – succeeded in establishing spas as unique spaces of hospitality that brought guests together for weeks on end. The long duration of the stay was itself legitimated to a large extent by the belief that the medicinal value of the waters of the spa could only be obtained through continuous exposure to them. Cures, it was claimed, took weeks to achieve (at times, requiring annual repetition), and doctors did what they could to provide evidence for this. At the same time, the duration of the stay (and the fact that it occurred during the warm summer months of the year) was also a significant factor contributing to the development of spas into vital spaces of leisure. While baths and taking the waters were the central activities around which cures were organized, this still left the larger part of the day to fill with content in the continuous struggle against boredom.

Leisure and the opening of hospitable spaces

In the end, it was perhaps here, in the hours between treatments, that the appeal of Swedish spas found its strongest foothold, because while the production of health was an important driving force behind the establishment of many of Sweden's oldest spas, it was not necessarily the most important factor that drew Sweden's upper classes to them in the eighteenth century, and facilitated their growth in popularity amongst the middle classes in the nineteenth century. At least as important for their development was the role they filled as arenas of play and social hospitality and interaction. From the very beginning the popularity of spas was dependent upon the fact that they constituted an important arena in which members of the upper classes could congregate, mingle, and meet.

Other such arenas existed in Sweden, but spas were slightly different due to the fact that they were seasonal (open for a short period of the year, over the course of the summer) and often geographically removed from the social environments in which the upper classes usually moved.

Here, the quality of the spa as a *destination* to which one traveled was in and of itself a significant factor facilitating the development and expansion of the spa phenomenon. In connection with this, an important part of the allure of the spa lay in the fact that it functioned as a public space of leisure open to women. At the time, women simply did not have the same possibilities to travel and move about in society as men did. A woman traveling by herself was easily marked as morally suspect – especially in the eyes of the upper and middle classes (Cocks 2001: 21; O'Dell 2004; Wolff 1995). This was the activity of prostitutes and tramps, not respectable women. In order to protect her reputation, a respectable woman on the move needed a chaperone or some form of guardian.

Spas proved to be highly adept at organizing themselves as hospitable spaces for upper-class women, and from the outset met the preconditions necessary to facilitate women's mobility. Among other things, they could extend living quarters to guests traveling with family members or groups of servants. Large communal dining halls, ballrooms, and reading rooms provided guests with spaces in which to socialize, move about in public, and make new acquaintances under controlled and observable conditions. And members of the clergy were always close by, holding daily prayer services and Sunday masses. Indeed, one of the first new words that the world of spas injected into the Swedish language was *brunnspredikan* ('spa sermon') which first appeared in 1680, following on the heels of the establishment of Sweden's very first spas (Mansén 2001). Swedish spas and religious moralities were always closely entwined (a theme explored more thoroughly in the next chapter). So if the medical pretexts for a spa visit were not sufficient to legitimate a stay and ensure the well-being of a woman's honor while attending the facility in the company of her 'protectors', perhaps the watchful eye of the spa's minister could work as an added assurance. In this sense, even if the freedom afforded to women here was limited, the spa environment nonetheless constituted one of the earlier openings of a hospitable space for them beyond the realms of the home.

But this was not necessarily a world weighed down by overbearing, pious finger-pointing. Alongside the minister's sermons lay a realm of possibilities for women and men alike. Most spas, for example, cultivated parks with winding paths, flowers, shrubs, trees, and scattered benches that could allow guests a rest from their walks, or provide them with a point from which to survey their surroundings. Small bands were employed to play music and entertain guests. Dances, balls, and masquerades were common events, as were card games, chess matches, and soirées that were arranged in reading rooms. And at most spas, amateur theater presentations were often arranged and performed by guests for their peers (Löfgren 1999: 110 ff.; Mansén 2005: 38 ff.). Having taken their cures, and attended morning prayer, it was possible for guests to wander, mingle, play, and interact as they waited for their next meal or treatment. This was a world in which it was possible for the upper classes to act in a carefree way that was usually not possible in the normal course of daily life (Löfgren 1989: 13 ff.). Herein lay a world of opportunities for the imagination to explore as guests played practical jokes on one another, threw secretive glances at potential suitors, exchanged greetings, and overheard the conversations of their neighbors. And this was a cultural climate that spas always tried to nurture.

In 1882, for example, the predecessor to *Ramlösa Hallået, Ramlösa Brunns- och Badtidning*, devoted half of its first page to a list of the people attending the spa that season. Listed here were Mayor von Sockenström, Doctor Appelgren, Professor Engelsted, Consul Westrup, Dean Hammar, Doctor of Philosophy Lindahl, Senior Enforcement Officer Ekelund, Music Director Lumbye, and so on (1882: 1). From today's perspective, the publication of a list of visitors to a resort may seem odd. But this was the equivalent of an address book of the 'who's who' at the resort at the time. Noticeably missing were the names of women, servants, maids, farmhands, and other people of lesser standing, whom, as the spa's guestbooks reveal, were the most prevalent groups of patrons in the late nineteenth century. The newspaper's list, while selective, clearly let people of standing know that they were in good company. This served several purposes. First, a list of prominent guests worked well for promotional purposes – allowing a spa to establish its position as a leisure space for those of means. In the process this increased the ability of the spa to attract other guests of standing (Mansén 2001: 67 & 2005: 42). And finally, in establishing itself as a hospitable space for such guests, it even served to reinforce the image of the spa as a social landscape of possibilities.[7]

Amongst these possibilities, love and courtship were one of the more popular themes of spa lore. In this sense, the story mentioned in the beginning of this chapter, of Aina, the young woman who fell in love with a fellow guest, only to have her heart broken, was rather common. The spa's facilities, with its parks, dining halls, bath houses and social rooms, provided ample opportunity for chance meetings under controlled conditions. The parks, while generally open to surveying eyes, could potentially provide a young couple with smaller spaces along secluded paths of overgrown shrubbery in which to exchange whispers, or even a kiss. In a similar manner, the balls, concerts, and theater performances taking place at these resorts offered young couples the opportunity to meet and socialize in a wide range of contexts over the course of their stay. In short, while dealing in health, the popularity of spas as summer destinations was tightly entangled in their ability to offer guests of standing a diverse leisure environment filled with activities in which to combine pleasure, mobility, and relaxation with small doses of social ambition and amorous adventure. This was an atmosphere that encouraged playfulness while simultaneously prescribing and encouraging guests to maintain a degree of tolerance to one another. In this sense, the ability of the spa to act as an early free zone for cultural experimentation in collective forms of play and leisure for the upper classes was central to the establishment of its reputation as a hospitable space for these guests.

Commercializing hospitality

Yet in Sweden, while spas first found an economic impetus for their early development in the upper classes, they progressively found that this small segment of the Swedish population was insufficient to sustain their existence. If spas were to survive in Sweden, they would need to find new groups of patrons. The burgeoning middle classes offered a solution. Here was a large and diverse group of potential guests with growing economic resources and matching aspirations for social advancement. For the middle classes, gaining access to the world of spas represented a movement into a new future of upward mobility and Continental tastes. For spas, this was an opportunity they could not afford to miss – and they did not.

Over the course of the nineteenth century, spas came to increasingly focus their attention upon attempts to attract members of the middle classes to their facilities. As part of this, they developed a multitude of special mid-priced package deals for these prospective patrons. For example, at Varberg Hafskuranstalt, a spa located on the west coast of Sweden, south of Gothenburg, a first-class guest paid a fee of 15 crowns for full access to the spa's facilities and services in 1888. Second-class guests paid a smaller fee of 5 crowns, which provided them with access to the facility's park, bathing veranda, and second-class baths, but did not provide them with the right to access the lounges, assembly rooms, reading rooms, soirées, or first-class baths (Levertin 1990: 64f.).

At Ramlösa Hälsobrunn, sources from the same period portray a similar but slightly more intensive situation. In addition to repeated visits by the king and Swedish royal family, Ramlösa came to attract the aristocracy of Scania (Skåne), many of whom built their own summer homes around the spa (Mansén 2001). And while these visitors made private contributions to the spa,[8] and organized balls, concerts, and theater performances -- the proceeds from which were donated to the spa (*Ramlösa Hallået* 1899: 5 & 1912: 7) – these contributions usually did not account for more than a sixth of the spa's annual income (Mansén 2001: 86). In order to make ends meet, the private owners of the spa found it necessary to attract the middle and lower classes through a process of diversification: building special ballrooms and living quarters for them, as well as organizing balls, fireworks, and carnivals. The management at Ramlösa even petitioned the king for the right to open a casino, and although permission was never granted, they nonetheless opened a highly popular gambling hall with card-tables and roulette wheels that not only attracted the spa's seasonal guests, but even drew Danes from across the Sound, who flocked to the facility on Sundays to place their bets (Lindblad 1907: 35 ff.; Norlind 1902: 14).

Nonetheless, these and other efforts to attract new groups of guests to Ramlösa Hälsobrunn were not enough to prevent the facility from facing constant economic problems that prompted regular changes in ownership. The question from a management perspective was, 'What should we do next?' It is against the relief of this precarious situation that the implications of the moral landscape of the day come more clearly into perspective. For despite the constant economic pressures that the spa met, it continuously made efforts to extend its hospitality to the poor and those who were less well-off. In part, a policy of openness and tolerance was prescribed by older patriarchal traditions and a sense of responsibility. In Sweden, for example, taking the waters was indelibly defined as an activity open to everyone, from the wealthiest to the most destitute members of society.[9] This remained the case at Ramlösa Hälsobrunn throughout the nineteenth century (Mansén 2001: 505). However, the extension of hospitality to the disenfranchised did not end there, as it perhaps could have in light of the economic difficulties and climate of growing economic rationalization that faced the spa.

Instead, efforts continued to be made to help those in need. On average, Ramlösa received approximately a thousand visitors per season in the early and mid-nineteenth century. But in a year such as 1835, 402 of these visitors received some form of economic support from the spa for their stay. This help tended to take the form of smaller subventions that covered the costs of the baths, food, housing, or medicines of those who could not afford them, but later came to be consolidated into a more limited number of full-season cures (five to six weeks) for those deemed to be in greatest need (Lindblad 1907: 49). And as a central aspect of this attempt to extend aid to the poor, the spa maintained a hospital devoted to their care.[10] In short, while Ramlösa attracted the upper echelons of the social and economic elite in southern Sweden, it also remained a rather heterogeneous environment in which very different groups of guests, visitors, and staff (including maids, bath maids, masseuses, cooks and attendants, who remained as inconspicuous as possible) moved around in proximity to one another, and in which the moral atmosphere of the times still prescribed a degree of tolerance on the part of guests that not only made this form of hospitality possible, but even compelling. Indeed, the maintenance of an air of tolerance was facilitated by the belief that spa life should be lighthearted, and free of haughtiness. Guests were quite simply expected to socialize and interact in ways that played down their differences in status (Mansén 2005: 41).

However, the emphasis of analysis should perhaps be placed upon the issue of proximity rather than tolerance. For while the socio-economic mix of guests at Ramlösa was diverse, guests from different social strata were by and large strangers to one another, and remained so throughout the course of their stay.[11] In this context, the routines, rules, and physical organization of the spa helped to minimize contact between different categories of spa guests. Taking the waters, for example, was an activity in which most guests participated, but the schedule was organized so that the poorest and most decrepit patients arrived at the spa's well early in the morning (at some spas this could mean getting up as early as 2 a.m.), while guests of higher standing arrived later in the day. In a similar manner, the existence of first- and second-class bath houses, living and medical facilities for the poor, special ballrooms and dance locations for the peasantry, privately owned summer-houses for the wealthy, and finer ballrooms and reading rooms for the cultural elite, all contributed to a pattern of perpetual motion in which guests circulated and socialized within circles constituted of patrons of similar standing. In this sense, the ability to maintain an assemblage of steering mechanisms, a 'social smoothing machine' of sorts (Bogard 2000: 272 ff., after Deleuze & Guattari 1987: 474 ff.), that minimized the friction between different categories of guests even as they moved around in proximity to one another, was integral to the cultural organization and production of hospitality and well-being at Ramlösa.

This is important because while pure hospitality necessitates a condition of unconditionality (Derrida 2000: 25), most forms of hospitality as we know and experience them are conditioned by cultur-ally bound codes and laws. In conditional hospitality the production of hospitable space not only required degrees of tolerance, but also, as Mustafa Dikeç has argued, acceptance and recognition (2002: 236). Unfortunately, cultural atmospheres that perpetuate attitudes of acceptance toward the Other can be fragile. Hospitable space is not something that can simply be created once and for all; it has to be opened and reopened, continuously made and remade. The case may be that this not only requires mechanisms that facilitate attitudes of acceptance, but perhaps just as importantly, cultural practices that diminish tension and friction, and that thereby facilitate the recognition of alternative life circumstances by reducing the chances that people close the door of recognition to one another. At Ramlösa Hälsobrunn the practices of corporal movement that existed there worked in this way for a while, contributing to the perpetuation of a space of hospitality that allowed for degrees of mutual recognition and acceptance between groups of guests.

Yet as a site of conditional hospitality, Ramlösa Hälsobrunn always remained an ambivalent space of hospitality. It was a place in which some sectors of guests sought to raise funds for the inclusion of others, but often did so through social activities whose fees prevented the participation of those Others. And these activities were conducted in a context in which 'the benevolent' paid for the (first-class) right to nurture their own well-being without the intrusion of Others. From the perspective of the spa-owners, the morals of the day made it difficult to justify the full and automatic exclusion of any group of sickly patrons on solely economic grounds, but economic realities also placed constraints on the degree to which the spa's hospitality could be extended to those without sufficient means, while simultaneously reinforcing the importance attached to both the paying customer, and her/his potential charitable good-will. In the face of these tensions, the production of well-being (or at least the sensations of well-being) was intimately linked to the careful orchestration of each guest's mobility, and guests themselves (particularly those of good standing) participated actively – even taking the initiative at times – in the perpetuation of these processes of control and segregation.

As Roy Wood has argued (1994), actors in the hospitality industry still work to control the movements of their guests and the interactions between them. Unfortunately, little systematic attention has been paid to these mobility-bound processes, and the significance these have in relation to commercialized forms of hospitality. Instead, as other commentators have noted (Brotherton 1999: 168), efforts made by management theorists, particularly those working in the field of hospitality management, to problematize hospitality as a phenomenon have all too often fallen into the trap of either striving to delineate the contours of an industry, or skewing the focus of the discussion in the direction of the products delivered: food, beverages, accommodation, and entertainment. This is not to say that hospitality management researchers have completely failed to acknowledge the guest–host relationship, or the fact that hospitality implicates processes of mobility – at least to the extent that some scholars have recognized that processes linked to issues of arrival and departure are important to understanding hospitality (see, for example, King 1995; Mullins 2001: 14) – but that these discussions have generally tended to be highly instrumental in nature. Rather than problematizing hospitality, they have all too often wound up offering models and methods for its 'deliverance'. Consequently, hospitality has been readily aligned with the provisioning of services, which are themselves fetishized as commodities with a definable exchange-and-use-value that can be optimized. In the process, hospitality seemingly becomes universally and democratically accessible as a market item. Questions which are comfortably avoided, and which I wish to draw attention to here, concern tolerance and the mechanisms by which commercialized institutions of hospitality such as spas, affect, sort, and categorize strangers, defining some as guests and some as employees, while disregarding those who are not present as irrelevant. In what ways are hospitable spaces opened, with which preconditions, and to whom?

Throughout the eighteenth century and early decades of the nineteenth century, spas proved to be the playground of the aristocracy. These were places in which dreams of romance could flourish as patrons strolled along the paths of the park, attended balls, dressed up and masqueraded around in costumes, or made small trips into the surrounding countryside (cf. Lagerqvist 1978: 56 ff.; Löfgren 1989). The medical pretexts under which spas were founded were important as a means culturally legitimating visits to them – even

47

if many of the people who came to these places lacked any serious affliction – and were one of the factors which helped *open* spas to women. These pretexts also played a central role in providing a structure to the stay that helped define its duration (of several weeks) and rhythm (with longer periods of time between treatments in which guests had to find ways of entertaining themselves). Herein lay the basic framework within which spas would be able to develop as spaces of hospitality.

But as Derrida, Dikeç, and others have pointed out, to speak of hospitality is to speak of openings, borders, and the ambivalences embedded in the word's Latin root, *hostis*; the ambivalences of the relationship between the guest (the enemy, even) and the host.[12] In this connection spas did much more than provide visitors with housing and shelter. They provided upper-class guests with a temporary home from home to which they could return year after year. But it was a home they shared with others: taking the waters together, eating meals together, laughing together, walking together, and dancing together. Daily life here was organized according to slightly different rules than those which applied at home. They encouraged a form of openness between guests that was essential to the maintenance of the social atmosphere that made spas feel so hospitable. This was a place in which one could lower one's guard slightly, and in which one was expected to do so. But in appropriating the spa as a home from home, the upper classes also took upon themselves part of the role of the host, of welcoming, tolerating, and supporting Others. This was part of the custom of the day, and after all, the coexistence of the local peasantry at the spa could easily be tolerated since there was never any risk that the aristocracy and elites of the time could be confused with those of much humbler origins.

The intensified commercialization of this field of leisure in the later nineteenth century complicated matters, however. Spas came to constitute one of the earlier tourist destinations for a widening mass of middle- and upper-class patrons. These were places in which visitors came to stay for weeks on end, and in which communities of acquaintances continued to take form. People got to know one another, and in some cases even came to expect to meet one another year after year. Newspapers such as *Ramlösa Hallået* were appreciated and purchased in this context not just because they represented a symbolic means for the middle classes to support those coming from less fortunate circumstances, but more importantly because guests could recognize one another's names and thereby more greatly appreciate the inside jokes and puns that the paper's contributors directed towards both one another and the entire spa experience in general. In this sense, it further facilitated a sense of community and belonging that came to be an important ingredient in the mix of hospitality that late-nineteenth century spas offered in Sweden.

But a growing sense of community amongst the spa's bourgeois clientele was not necessarily a phenomenon equally appreciated by all. While the aristocracy may not have felt socially threatened by the co-existence of destitute local peasants at the spa, the introduction of growing numbers of other groups of culturally and economically endowed patrons was potentially more problematic. Creating a space of hospitality here required that spas were capable of rethinking themselves. It was no longer enough to provide guests with housing, food, and a multitude of leisure opportunities – the basic components to a spa stay that the aristocracy expected to receive in the eighteenth century – but to do so in degrees. Ultimately, this would provide guests with a means of distinguishing themselves from one another, while simultaneously allowing spas to attract and accommodate a broader group of guests.

Working against this background of cultural and economic pressures, spas quickly became adept at rethinking hospitality in increments. If the first-class package included access to specific bathing, living, and entertainment facilities, then the second-class package implicitly meant rethinking these offerings in terms of less. But the hospitality of spas was intricately linked to the provision of care, solicitude, and medical attention. It was one thing to construct simpler ballrooms and bathing facilities for second-class guests (or build newer and more modern facilities for first-class guests), but how did one provide less than full medical attention to ailing and paying guests? The answer, as the schedule for taking the waters illustrates, came, at least in part, in the form of less convenience – but at the end of the day, less convenience translated into less care.

At the time, nobody thought of Swedish spas in terms of a 'hospitality industry', but an outcome of the activities taking place here would ultimately contribute to our way of thinking of hospitality in degrees, increments, and units: degrees of value and convenience; increments of luxury, pampering, and service; and units of equivalency in which economic units could be translated into the rights to specific forms of treatment and care. For guests of the time this not only led to different rhythms of movement for different groups of guests, but even an ability to distinguish between guests as they moved about. And it implied learning the implicit rules of maneuvering around the borders of the spa – of learning how to move about in the right places, amongst the right people, and in a manner that seemed unproblematic and carefree. The hospitality of the spa was never opened equally to all, but the borders of the spa, and the manner in which it opened itself to its guests, became increasingly intricate over time. In the process, the expectations that different classes of guests had of the hospitality of the spa became increasingly diverse. Interestingly, all of this ultimately occurred in a manner that would come to be seen as only 'natural'. However, an awareness of the history of spas helps remind us of the degree to which the activities we partake in – and which we all too readily regard as the 'natural way of doing things' – are culturally learned. Indeed, the history presented here will be discussed further in the coming chapters of this book for a similar reason. The past, as it turns out, works well as a foil against which to view the present, helping us gain distance and new perspectives on much of that which we take for granted in the present.

Demise and rebirth

In the end, most spas in Sweden fell on hard times in the twentieth century, and all but disappeared after the Second World War. Some survived by working with physical therapy and rehabilitation programs in conjunction with the local municipal health care system, some became health farms, some established themselves as conference centers, and some hobbled along as summer vacation destinations (cf. Mansén 2001: 50 & 2005: 75 ff.; Vik 1995: 9). But for the most part, the majority of Swedish spas closed their doors one after the other. Ramlösa Brunn proved to be one of the long-term survivors, but even Ramlösa Brunn descended ultimately into bankruptcy and was finally forced to close in the 1970s. The glory days of Swedish spas appeared to be over, their reputations seemingly tarnished beyond repair. After all, a visit to a health farm or rehabilitation center was fine if you had a problem, but this was hardly an environment which appealed to most Swedes as a vacation destination, or a place for ordinary relaxation in the late twentieth century. And the appeal of the type of collective vacation in which everyone ate together and mingled with one another, day in day out, had come to feel somewhat antiquated for the middle and upper classes. The spas which still existed as the millennium came to a close seemed to be living on borrowed time.

However, history has a way of unraveling in unexpected ways. In the late 1990s the few spas that remained found themselves receiving growing numbers of visitors. At first the increases were incremental, but by the early years of the twenty-first century Swedish spas found their revenues increasing by as much as 50–75 per cent a year.[13] And hotels that did not have spa facilities scurried to build them. Nevertheless, as the Swedish spa industry grew in this period, it also transformed itself, as spa managers endeavored to distance themselves from their tainted health farm image. Brochures featuring elegant dinners with wine and well-stocked bars became standard course for actors in the industry. And where visitors once came to spas to spend the summer and meet old acquaintances, spas now specialized in providing overnight packages and weekend getaways for couples. The old collectivities that were once one of the appealing attractions of older spas were replaced by couples and individuals who were inwardly focused upon themselves and each other. In this sense, the years of dearth that Swedish spas encountered in the late twentieth century worked to separate them from their older eighteenth- and nineteenth-century roots and traditions. Spas in the twenty-first century would create a niche for themselves as sanctuaries from burn-out, capable of working a type of magic that could counter the effects of stress and life on the go.

The hospitality that they promise to extend to their patrons is still embedded in a discourse of wellness that provides the superficial appearance of a linkage to the past, but upon closer reflection, a critical awareness of the historical context out of which Swedish spas have evolved makes clear that the conditions through which this is achieved have changed dramatically. Where spas once promoted themselves as arenas of social interaction in which well-being could be achieved through the outer effects of doctors and personnel in combination with the interaction of the patient and the surrounding social and physical environment, Swedish spas now market themselves as places that produce experiences of well-being that emanate from within – albeit with the aid of others, in a specific material environment, and through the orchestration of new modes of mobility. In the process, their orientation has shifted, as has the form of hospitality they strive to offer their guests, from a context of trying to bring people together to one that endeavors to create isolated spaces of reflection. Here we find new linkages between current interests in personal health, the consumption and production of experiences (cf. O'Dell & Billing 2005; Pine and Gilmore 1999), and the offerings of the hospitality industry. In the following chapter I shall examine these linkages more closely, and focus upon the promises made by modern Swedish spas, and the ways in which they work to fulfill their promises.

CHAPTER 3

Magic, Ritual, and the Mass Production of Serenity

A lone stone. The pure lines of a sofa. We have designed Yasuragi in line with Japanese aesthetics in which *wabi* represents that which is simple, and *sabi* is the hard to describe elegance which you find in an old, small object. In order to create a harmonious wholeness in which energy flows in the right way, we've taken advice from a *feng-shui master*. (Yasuragi brochure *Sinnesro*, undated: 5)

One of the most damaging ideas that has swept the social sciences and humanities has been the idea of a disenchanting modernity… This act of purification has radically depopulated thinking about Western societies as whole sets of delegates and intermediaries have been consigned to oblivion as extinct impulses, those delegates and intermediaries which might appear to be associated with forces of magic, the sacred, ritual, affect, trance and so on … [However] magic has not gone away. Western societies, like all others, are full of these forces. (Thrift, 2000b: 44)

In January 2002, *Spa Magazine* made its debut on Swedish news-stands. In the coming issues readers would find articles informing them about everything from 'healing waters' and 'magical mud' to the exotic rituals of the Japanese bath offered by Hasseludden Conference & Yasuragi, a spa-like conference center located outside Stockholm.

First, you wash your body. With calm rhythmic motions you scrub your skin clean and let several buckets of water rinse the dirt and soap away. After that, it's time for your soul. With the same motions you wash away everything that is lying there, chafing and pressing against you unnecessarily. (*Spa Magazine* 2002: 25)

This was an exotic world quite different from that encountered by most people in the course of their daily routines. In many ways it was a sensual world bordering on the mystical, magical, and spiritual. In other ways the magazine revealed the contours of a highly profane world in which advertisers struggled to sell consumers health, well-being, and relaxation in an array of products, including oils, lotions, and skin-care products. Even airlines were in on the game. Icelandair, for example, promoted 'The Icelandic Spa Cocktail … Add equal parts of pleasure, enjoyment and good food. The result? A weekend full of experiences you will never forget' (Icelandair advertisement 2002: 40). Included in their package was a beauty treatment at 'Planet Pulse, where well-being and relaxation are keywords' and a bathing trip to the 'unique Blue Lagoon' which, as it happens, is a cooling tank at a geothermal heating plant located in a barren lava field outside of Reykjavik.

The market for tranquility, relaxation, and well-being surrounding us today is enormous and diverse, but the mass production of serenity requires more than a little magic of its own. Obviously, not all the actors hurrying into this market are equally suited to succeed here. How do Swedish spas currently work to open a space of hospitality for their guests, given that it rests precariously in a field of cultural tension constituted by processes of mass-production on the one side, and the desire to achieve individual well-being on the other? How are actors who have positioned themselves in this market to attract customers and meet their needs? How is 'well-being' produced on a mass scale? And what type of magic is required to transform a broken down, stressed-out, and exhausted middle-aged couple into a rejuvenated, relaxed, and revitalized conjugal pair – all over the course of a weekend?

In order to approach these questions, this chapter is grounded in empirical material primarily taken from three spas – Varberg Kurort Hotel & Spa, Hasseludden Conference & Yasuragi, and Varberg Stads Hotel and Asia Spa[1] – and the cultural context in which they operate. As I shall demonstrate, the world of modern Swedish spas is one that has increasingly come to invoke metaphors of spirituality, rejuvenation, and obscure magical processes that are said to be capable of unleashing 'hidden flows of energies' from within (and around) the body. Against this background, I shall intentionally press the concept of magic, and use it as a prism through which to view these spas.

I will argue that magic and magical processes are alive and well in Western society, despite the predominant contemporary belief to the contrary. The chapter proceeds after this by presenting the contours of Marcel Mauss' theory of magic that will be used to frame the discussion which follows. Taking inspiration from Mauss, the text then investigates the promises that spas make to their guests, and the manner in which they strive to fulfill them, as they take buildings of generally profane origins and convert them into sanctuaries for the transformation of souls and bodies. After this, the chapter analyzes the 'magical rites', and 'magical representations' (aspects of magic that Mauss identified as central to any understanding of magic [2001: 23]) that spas work with to achieve their goals while meeting and forming their guests' expectations. My argument here is that while a focus upon the processes involved in the making of sanctuaries and conducting of magic, as well as the rites and representations that are needed to perform magic, may seem to fly in the face of common sense (or at least a view of the world that most people claim to hold), it may actually be a necessary step to take if we are to understand the dynamics of spas and the cultural economy we live in today.[2]

In modern society, most people would distance themselves from any claim in the belief of magic or its existence. To speak of magic is (seemingly) to speak of that which is illogical, irrational, and wholly delusional.[3] It is an act which flies in the face of the reason and lessons of science. But as many scholars have pointed out (Greenwood 2000 & 2005; Pels 2003; Thrift 2000b), we still live in a time filled with that which is magical, mystical and spiritual. As Nigel Thrift has argued:

> We live in an age … in which many people still take astrology seriously, and many others at least take note of it … in an age in which near-death experience has its own academic journals and death still has its very definite rituals, in an age in which older religious traditions like New Thought, Theosophy, Spiritualism stirred and

shaken by the psychological and Eastern religious imaginings of the 1950s and 1960s countercultures, have seen a rebirth as New Age…The whole fabric of everyday life, in other words, is shot through with dreams, fantasies, superstitions, religious yearnings and millenarian movements. *The magic has not gone away.* (Thrift 1996: 165, emphasis in the original)

Indeed, rather than disappearing, it seems as though magic has actually been on the move just below the radar of much of the work being done in the social sciences. But this situation is changing, and thus, while it is commonly asserted that Western society is secularized, a growing number of scholars are calling attention to the fact that the situation may be more complicated than this generalization would lead us to believe. For example, Collin Campbell has drawn attention to the manner in which New Age and Eastern philosophies have been on the rise in Britain in recent decades – contributing to a process which he refers to as a spiritual 'Easternization of the West'. As he explains:

The percentage of the population who say that they believe in God has been steadily falling since Gallup began regular polling on this question after the Second World War … However, this apparently straightforward evidence for secularization disguises the fact that this decline has been entirely at the expense of belief in the Western Judaeo-Christian conception of a personal God. … By contrast, [the] proportion prepared to admit to a belief in 'some sort of spirit or life-force' has actually increased slightly in recent years. (Campbell 1999: 36)

In other words, while the degree to which people in many Western societies participate in traditional, organized, and collective forms of religion is on the decline, there is evidence that they are not simply 'giving up' on the realm of the spiritual (cf. Hutchinson 2006: 10), but are looking for new places and forms of faith in which to invest their beliefs. Eastern philosophies and their hybridized New Age reinterpretations are, according to Campbell, of central importance as a part of this process.

To be sure, the lessons of the Enlightenment have left their mark on much of modern society, but, despite this, maybe the 'laws of science' have not totally eradicated all 'irrational' thought and belief from daily life (cf. Hutchinson 2006: 10). The case may be that despite all claims to the contrary, we need a little bit of magic in our lives to make sense out of the world around. Perhaps not everything around us is so easily explained through appeals to logic and reason. But if any of this is true, it still leaves open the question of how we might understand the concept of magic. In order to approach this question, I would like to turn to the work of Marcel Mauss.

A general theory of magic

The goal is a healthier and more complete life. Increased well-being, better balance, less detrimental stress, and a greater flow of energy. At our spa you can find serenity, relaxation, and luxury.[4]

Magic is essentially the art of doing things, and magicians have always taken advantage of their know-how, their dexterity, their manual skill. Magic is the domain of production *ex nihilo*. (Mauss 2001: 175)

In 1902 Mauss first published *A General Theory of Magic*, in which he surveyed the manner in which peoples around the world, and in different times, used, controlled, and understood magic. Magic proved to be an object of study that presented the ethnologist with special problems. As he explained, 'Magic is an institution only in the most weak sense; it is a kind of totality of actions and beliefs, poorly defined, poorly organized even as far as those who practice it and believe in it are concerned' (2001: 13). It was, in his view, a phenomenon uncomfortably located in the tension-filled borderland between religion, science, and technology. Its existence necessitated two different forms of belief that he called a 'will to believe' and 'actual belief' (2001: 117).

On the one hand, magicians often work with different techniques of sleight of hand that only they understand and are aware of. They know, for example, that when pulling foreign objects out of people's bodies, they themselves are manipulating those objects in a way that creates the appearance – like an adult who can miraculously pull candy out of a child's ear. However, on the other hand, amongst 'true magicians'[5] this knowledge is coupled with a 'will to believe' in the power of the magic they manipulate as well as an actual belief in those magical powers. This is necessary because in the end there can be no magic – and it can have no effect – without large numbers of people who actually believe in it, and are willing to believe in it. As Mauss phrased it, 'Magic, like religion, is viewed as a totality; either you believe in it all, or you do not' (2001: 113).

The similarity with religion also extends to the way in which magic tends to be organized as a ritualized activity involving specific rites, spirits, and incantations. But magic is also, in Mauss' view, the forbear of science and technology. It is, as he argues, the field of activity through which nature was first explored and classified as the properties and secrets of plants, animals, and inanimate objects in the surrounding world were scrutinized. It is here, Mauss argues, that medicine and astronomy have their roots (2001: 176 ff.).

Understood in this way, magic has nothing to do with the hocus-pocus of the Houdinis and David Copperfields of the world. Such people may be illusionists – people who misdirect our gaze, focus, and orientation – but they are not magicians. No one believes that Copperfield is doing what he claims to do; we simply enjoy the fact that he is, despite all our attempts to reveal him, able to deceive us. Magic is subsumed in a cultural context in which people want to believe, and end up doing so. It is a cutting edge along which new technologies are explored and experimented with, but also one along which old technologies are combined and manipulated in new ways to meet new ends. The question in the case of spas is how is this done, and is it possible that an appreciation of the phenomenon of magic can help us understand the cultural economy of this small section of a rapidly growing health sector?

Profane openings into the realm of rejuvenation

Magic is not performed just anywhere, but in specially qualified places. Magic as well as religion has genuine sanctuaries. (Mauss 2001: 57)

The three spas that this chapter focuses upon are large facilities that include living and eating accommodations, as well as a wide assortment of massages, treatments, and activities. In addition to this, all three of these establishments have invested heavily in the development of conference facilities. Consequently, their clientele include not only private parties, but to a large extent they are also dependent upon business customers who use these spas as larger meeting places. These are rather large spa facilities by Swedish standards, and similar in this sense; nonetheless, they are also quite different in the way they present themselves and strive to please their customers.

Varberg Kurort has 106 rooms, and is located on the Swedish west coast just south of Gothenburg. Its reputation as a health resort dates back to the early nineteenth century. At various times throughout most of the twentieth century the facility has also functioned as a sanatorium and rehabilitation center. Still to this day the spa offers medical services and numbers nurses and physiotherapists alongside its other personnel of masseurs, therapists, and trainers. Varberg's Kurort is interesting in this context because it is arguably one of Sweden's most medically oriented spa facilities, and in this sense one might presume one of the most unlikely spas in which to find magic.

Echoing its past, the facility's main building clearly reflects the early modern esthetics found in most hospitals and institutions built in the early portion of the twentieth century in Sweden. The main lobby, however, takes its cues from English aesthetics, including dark wooden floors, paneled wood walls, and deep green, stuffed leather furniture. As Mats, one of Varberg's managers explains: "It's quite funny, but many of the new guests who come here say that they feel a sense of serenity wash over them when they enter the lobby. And that's what a lot of people are striving for today, to calm down and relax." The spa's historic roots, twentieth-century institutional architecture, and classical English-style lobby all work together to create a calming atmosphere that sets the facility apart from many of the trendier newcomers on the spa scene. It does so by symbolically assuring visitors that this is an establishment rich in tradition, with a well-rooted heritage of its own that is itself coupled to a deeply anchored history of medical professionalism.

Hasseludden Conference & Yasuragi features 162 hotel rooms and

The English style lobby at Varberg Kurort with its green paneled wood walls and dark wooden floors. Photo: Tom O'Dell.

lies on the east coast of Sweden, in the Stockholm archipelago.[6] It was built in the early 1970s by the Swedish Trade Union Confederation, LO, with the intention of using the facility as a conference and educational center (Brink, undated: 153 ff.). In terms of its physical appearances, the building is influenced by Japanese architectural styles and aesthetics, and was designed by Yoji Kasajima. The Japanese theme permeating the building's architecture has been carried over into other realms of the spa's activities, including Japanese inspired treatments and massages, the Yasuragi bathing facilities,[7] several restaurants serving Japanese food, and the fact that guests are requested to wear traditional cotton Japanese robes, or *yukata*, throughout the duration of their stay.

Varberg's Asia Spa was built in 1902 in a style reminiscent of a large French chateau. Its red brick exterior dominates the central

At Varberg's Asia Spa, the art of converting a hotel attic into a sanctuary for relaxation lies in an attention to the details that is coupled with the liberal use of diverse symbols that lead the visitor's associations toward the Orient. Photo: Tom O'Dell.

square of Varberg. Inside, the hotel portion of the facility includes 123 guest rooms and suites which were renovated in a more modern style in 1997, although in order to fit in with the spa's Asian theme some of the rooms have been remodeled in a Japanese style, with futon-like beds and closet doors of rice-paper. In contrast, the lobby is still unmistakably a product of the early twentieth century. Upon entering it, guests are met by a large central staircase that leads up one flight before coming to a landing, from which two more flights of stairs lead up from both the left- and the right-hand side of the landing to the second floor. Just before this central staircase, the reception desk, made in massive dark wood, is set slightly to the left. To the right one finds the elevator leading up to the Asia Spa, on the top floor of the hotel.

Upon exiting the elevator, guests enter what was once the attic of the hotel, in which the rustic brick walls and wooden beams have been renovated and preserved carefully to create a muted impression. This is a feeling that is reinforced by the grey stone-like tiles and red oriental carpets that cover the floor, and which is further accentuated by the heavy red drapes hung on some of the walls. Buddha statues, oriental symbols, and wooden benches (that look as though they have come from feudal Japan) decorate the facility. At the end of a long dark corridor the spa opens up to two heated outdoor pools, and a large indoor pool featuring thirty different stations in which the water bubbles, flows, and shoots in jet streams to stimulate the body in different ways. In contrast to the rest of the spa, which is dimly lit, the pool room features glass walls and skylights that flood the room with sunlight during the day.

Promising the impossible?

None of these three spas were originally constructed to function as spas. Varberg Kurort was a sanatorium that was later used as a health resort and was converted into a conference center in the 1990s. Hasseludden was constructed as a conference and educational center.[8] And Varberg's Asia Spa was, up until the late 1990s, a rather traditional early twentieth-century small city hotel, aspiring to some of the pomp and glamor of the grand hotels of

Europe's big cities. Despite these profane roots, all three places now present themselves as sites in which special powers or energies can be gathered and stored in different ways. For example, in their gift certificates Varberg Kurort claims, 'A visit to Varberg Kurort is just as enjoyable as it is wholesome. Every cell in you relaxes and gathers strength. Your entire body will thank you. For a long time to come.'[9] In a similar vein, Varberg's Asia Spa explains that the 'Eastern traditions' that have inspired their activities and treatments work to achieve 'calm and harmony at the same time that they create new life force and energy' (*Varbergs Stadshotell & Asia Spa* 2006: 17). And in an elegant coffee-table book, full of color pictures, recipes, and articles about Japanese traditions, one of Hasseludden's former managers presents the spa with the following words: 'The idea is that our guests will shut out the outside world, and essentially do nothing. It is these types of moments in which you can catch your breath, which we need in our lives. It is in these moments that we *gather strength, refill our energies*, have time to reflect, and maybe learn to think from the inside out.' (Tryggstad, undated: 5, my emphasis)

The tendency to invoke a rhetorical discourse of flowing energies that can be harnessed and stored is not limited to spas. It reflects a deeper pattern in society today in which our bodies are metaphorically likened to magnets or batteries that can absorb and attract energy, be charged, recharged, and revitalized, or alternatively drained of energy, run-down, or burned-out. But in aligning themselves with this imagery, the spas, and others like them, position themselves as transfer stations of a sort, in which 'energies' and 'powers' can be moved and gathered from (or via) the resources of the spa and set in motion in the bodies of the spa's clientele. The problem here is that, unlike cell phones and lap-top computers, people are not equipped with rechargeable batteries. Spas, nonetheless, are tightly woven into the structures of this discourse and invoke its imagery liberally; they thus, in practice, have to produce the impossible in order to survive. They have to provide us with the sensation that we have been recharged.

The question is, how can a sanatorium, union conference center, and city hotel be made to deliver upon these promises? The answer,

The activities pool at Varberg's Asia Spa with its thirty stations of bubbling corporeal stimulation. Photo: Tom O'Dell.

I shall argue, is through a great deal of ritual and symbolic work. In order to illustrate how this actually works, the following sections of this chapter will focus upon an analysis of how these places engage one of the most central and important realms of magic production which Mauss called the 'rites of magic'. In this, the text moves in tandem with Mauss' own thinking, and proceeds through an analysis of the places, props, and performances of magic – in that order. All the while, the objective is to draw attention to the significance that issues of ritualization play in the staging and production of well-being.

The materiality of spell-casting: making sanctuaries

As Marcell Mauss argued (2001: 57), magic does not just occur anywhere. It needs its own sanctuaries to work, and along these lines spas go to great lengths to establish themselves as enclaves of disjuncture. The first and perhaps most obvious way in which they proceed to do this is through the delineation of explicit rules of conduct. Spas, as it turns out, might be places for relaxation, but they are also full of small signs, brochures, and 'Welcome Folders' that explicitly tell guests what they should and should not do. 'Please turn off your mobile phones', 'It is forbidden to dive into the pool', 'Please put your towels and robes in the basket when you are done with them', 'No shoes allowed', 'No one under the age of 16', and perhaps most importantly, 'Please remember that other guests might be having a massage or trying to enjoy a moment of relaxation, rest, and calm. For this reason, move slowly and speak softly'. These somewhat repetitious instructions are found in one form or another in most spas. In part they attest to the novelty of the spa experience. This is still a world of activity in which many guests are uncertain as to where the boundaries of correct spa etiquette might be drawn. Consequently, it is not unusual to hear them asking receptionists and personnel for information about what they should wear, how they should prepare for a treatment, and what they should expect from it. But in part, the existence of these printed instructions also reminds us that creating magic is not an easy task. Even the most unassuming of activities and sources of interaction can prove to be highly disenchanting: from the ring of a cell phone to a spontaneous dive into the pool.

The challenge that the spas I am describing here are faced with is not only that of providing guests with the feeling that they have left a world of problems and pressures behind them, but that they have even entered a new and somewhat special place that is empowered with a unique aura, potentially capable of healing stressed bodies and burned-out souls. Complicating matters, however, all of the spas I am addressing here are incorporated into hotel environments that include highly developed conference centers. The hustle and bustle of corporate life is never very far away.

The architectural layout and physical organization of the spa play an important role in facilitating the feeling that the spa is somehow distinctly separated from the normal pulse of daily life. In order to reach the spa facility at Varberg Kurort, for example, one has to move to the left through the lobby, and follow a long, narrow and winding corridor to the spa. The guests attending conferences will be led to the right, down another corridor that ultimately leads them to another building. At Varberg's Asia Spa, the physical separation of work and leisure is achieved in a similar manner, but in this case through the location of the spa on a floor of its own at the very top of the hotel. In both cases, the end result is not dramatically different from that which was described in the previous chapter in relation to Ramlösa and other nineteenth-century spas. Different categories of guests are separated, and kept moving in slightly different circles, even if their paths may cross at times in lunchrooms, lobbies, or other public areas.

More significantly, however, the architectural design of these spas is important due to the manner in which it symbolically frames the spa experience, and mediates the expectations of guests. As Medina Lasansky has pointed out in her discussion of the role architecture plays in leisure and tourism settings, buildings and spaces can be 'understood as a set of activities, products and attitudes that complement and complete both the design and meaning of specific sites' (2004: 3). In this regard, Varberg Kurort has an advantage. Its history as a sanatorium exudes an atmosphere of curative possibilities. And although a sanatorium may hardly seem to be a likely place in which to find magical processes, the medical history of the building is extraordinarily viscous (cf. Hetherington 2004: 162), constantly folding in upon the current spa environment, sticking to it, and providing it with a tangible aura of health production.[10]

This sensation is reinforced by the long, wide, ward-like corridor that meets guests as they pass the reception to the spa section of the facility. Here visitors who are visibly sick or disabled (including people who are wheelchair-bound as well as guests who have recently undergone chemotherapy) circulate amongst other guests who have come to be 'pampered, looked after, and cared for' (to use some of the most commonly invoked words of my informants). At the same time, uniformed staff members that include physical therapists, cognitive psychotherapists, dieticians, and masseuses circulate within the hall, looking for their next client and guiding them in the direction of the appropriate treatment room. Health, sickness, healing, and leisure are, in other words, embodied and lived by the very people inhabiting the corridor – it is nearly inescapable.

However, in order to diminish the 'hospital' feel of this hall, aspects of the facility's history have to be downplayed and esthetically disposed of. They have to be re-worked and architecturally put into an esthetic state that is akin to what Kevin Hetherington has referred to as 'secondhandedness' (Hetherington 2004). That is, even as the esthetics harkening back to the facility's history as a sanatorium are played upon and re-invoked to create an atmosphere of professional health-care, they are reframed and re-loaded with meaning in ways that down play aspects of that history. A number of strategies are used to achieve this goal. For example, stylized barriers have been erected in the middle of the corridor as a means of softening the no-nonsense linearity of the ward hall. These barriers are made of dark slatted wood and have a curved flowing form that breaks up the stringent rationalized architectural form of the hospital corridor. They do not extend all the way up to the ceiling, but high enough to inhibit the ability of visitors to see all the way down the corridor, making it feel shorter, but still open and airy. The feeling of the English-inspired lobby lingers on into the spa section of the facility via the ashen-green color in which the lobby wall paneling is painted. In the spa, this same color adorns the doors leading to the showers, changing rooms, and baths along the main corridor, as well as the wall trimming. As one moves from the hotel lobby to the spa, however, the signification of this color changes slightly. While the color is intended to create an 'English' feel to the lobby, its continued use in the hospital-like corridor of the spa produces associations that feel increasingly less English, and more Swedish. The reason for this is that the shade of ashen-green used throughout the facility is similar to a shade that Swedes associate to the National Romantic painter Carl Larsson (and which is known as 'Carl Larsson green'). It is, in other words, a color associated with the warmth of the home as well as nostalgic feelings of an age of Swedish peasantry gone by. Ultimately, the color setting of the hallway interacts with the early twentieth-century architectural details found here to produce a nostalgic resonance of warmth and tranquility.

The process of transformation is further facilitated by more modern, but intentionally understated changes that have been built into (and along) the corridor, such as a hair salon with modern fogged windows that prevent passing visitors from looking in, but which allow daylight

Frosted windows along the corridor of Varberg Kurort's spa allow sunlight to seep into the spa, providing a muted and welcoming feeling of warmth. Photo: Tom O'Dell.

to pass though into the hall in a soft and muted fashion. Nearby, a water cooler – harkening upon the roots of the spa tradition – provides guests with the opportunity of a drink. And across the hall, a gift shop opens up to a larger heated indoor salt-water pool featuring wooden lounge chairs, white marble Greek statutes, small trees, and large floor-to-ceiling windows that help provide the room with a warm feeling as the sunlight pours through the windows.

Many of the changes to the corridor may seem cosmetic at best – a layer of paint here, a water cooler and lounge chair there – but they seem to work. For example, when one woman whom I spoke with tried to explain why she preferred Varberg Kurort to another, more modern spa in the area, she explained: "Because it's a little more, it feels a little more, what should I say? It feels a little bit more like home. Things are very formal and clinical at [the other west-coast spa]."[11] Endowing a sanatorium with a feeling of home is not necessarily an easy task, but the key to success here lies in finding the right mix of symbols that can transform one history (that of the sanatorium) into another (through associations with National Romanticism) and merge them with a present context of well-being that guests find meaningful. In doing this, however, Varberg Kurort does not constitute itself as just any home; it is a home with a tradition of medical attention and corporeal transformation. And this history has a haunting effect as it reverberates throughout the facility, filling it (as well as those who move about within its perimeters) with a nearly tangible ambiance of professional care that is central to Varberg Kurort's ability to assert itself as a sanctuary of change and stress relief (cf. Hetherington 2002: 170).

The cultural organization of sanctuaries of this sort can, however, work in very different ways from one setting to the other. Varberg's Asia Spa works from a radically different set of preconditions: the attic of an early twentieth-century hotel. Here guests wander the dimly lit corridors wearing rubber sandals and black *yukatas* (with a white Chinese symbol printed on the back), and carrying small wicker baskets containing paper drinking cups and wash-cloths. The shower rooms feature small, foot-high wooden stools upon which guests are expected to sit as they wash themselves, rinsing the soap from their bodies by pouring water over their heads from small wooden buckets that appear to have their stylistic origins in south-east Asia. Some of the walls in the spa are made from rice-paper. Rooms for relaxation and meditation feature wicker or 'aged' wooden furniture, small Buddha figures, and futons neatly placed on the floor and adorned with pillows. The window sills in the spa are decorated with either small Asian-style vases containing plants that also appear to be Asian in origin, or simple arrangements of stones. All the while, the Asian theme plays upon the notion of stripping away all that is excessive, of returning to a purer aesthetic and perhaps even spiritual state.

The alignment of the spa's activities with the flow of spiritual energy is heightened in part by burning incenses, darkened corridors, rustic brick walls, and exposed wooden beams that all work together to produce a temple-like atmosphere. But they are further enhanced by a series of New Age references. Accordingly, much of the spa is acoustically furnished with New Age music featuring chanting, drums, and chimes. Books on meditation are available in relaxation rooms, free to be read or thumbed through should guests feel so inclined. Pillows and mattresses are laid out on the floors of these rooms, almost calling out to bodies, encouraging them to assume a more informal, down-to-earth position that temporarily resists the world of chairs, tables, and desks. Blankets lie neatly folded on the mattresses, or carefully stacked in small piles on the floor by the pillows, further accentuating the welcoming appeal of these floor-bound spaces. And drapery is used to divide some of the larger relaxation rooms into smaller, more privately compartmentalized 'soft spaces' for rest or inward reflection. Not everyone necessarily assumes the lotus position, but the material arrangement of these rooms has an inhibiting and dampening effect upon those who move around within them. People remain silent, or speak in hushed voices. Eye contact with strangers is avoided, as is physical proximity. This may be a hotel attic, but it feels like a shrine, and for the most part people move about within it as if it were a holy place.

In the book *Wild Things*, Judy Attfield argues for the need to view textiles as a special form of material culture. As she explains,

> textiles present a particularly apposite object type to illustrate how things are used to mediate the interior mental world of the individual, the body and the exterior objective world beyond the self through which a sense of identity is constructed and transacted in social relations. (2000: 123)

Cloth has a nearly ephemeral quality. Like a fluid, it can readily shift shape, position, and appearance as it flows, flutters, and folds in upon itself. Strings and threads do the same thing, but cloths and textiles do more than this because they are composite ensembles of threads, strings, and fibers that have been woven together. Together, in the form of cloth, they encompass the body, enwrap it, and constitute a direct and intimate interface between it and the surrounding world. In the process they destabilize the subject–object dichotomy as they conjoin 'the interior mental world of the individual, the body and the exterior objective world', as Attfield phrases it (ibid.). In arguing this point, she critically questions the propensity of many scholars in the field of cultural studies to read material culture in general (and textiles and clothing specifically) as though they were texts. More than having a textuality that can be read from a distance, clothes and fabrics have a materiality and (what she calls) 'textility' that work directly upon the body.

In a sense, it might be argued that in addition to the viscous history employed by Varberg Kurort, the materiality of both Varberg Kurort and Varberg's Asia Spa includes elements that are akin to the notion of *textility* that Attfield brings to our attention. True, if the material culture of these places is read and deconstructed on an item-by-item basis, the magic of the atmospheres they strive to produce can quickly be dispelled. One does not, for example, have to scrutinize the Buddha statues at Varberg's Asia Spa for very long to realize that these are decontextualized mass-produced objects that have found a niche for themselves as decorative commodities in spas around the world – flip through any spa magazine and these Buddha statues seem to be everywhere. But reading spas in this way misses the manner in which they create an overall impression, albeit using rather simple means; it misses the significance played by the overall contextual feeling of the spas. Or to rework Attfield's discussion, it misses the *contextility* of the spa experience, and the manner in which ensembles of material objects and architectural cues work together to convert rather mundane environments into more fabric-like experiences that enwrap, engulf, and engage the body and senses. In addition to this, a distanced deconstruction of the spa risks missing the potential ability that material culture has to take on an agency of its own, reaching into people and moving them in ways that cannot be explained easily through logical 'readings' of the world around us (Miller 2001: 112). There are processes at work here – with magical and haunting qualities of their own – that defy such logical and distanced analyses.

Magical rites and production *ex nihilo*

In short, with a very limited amount of time at their disposal (often not more than a day or two) spas have to use all the means at their disposal to quickly 'recharge' their guests and provide them with a sense of feeling better. It is important to understand the material organization of the spa, I would argue, because it constitutes one of the most central preconditions out of which guests' perceptions of their stay begin to take form. If magic does require the existence of 'special places' in which it can be produced, as Mauss argued (2001: 57), then an appreciation of the material arrangement of the spa is fundamental to an understanding of the cultural work-ings of the spa. But the materiality of the spa goes beyond issues of architecture, interior design, and thematic furnishings which guests encounter as they move about within the confines of the spa. It is even implicated in the *rites of affectation* to which guests' bodies are continuously exposed. In order to examine these rites of affectation more closely, it is time to leave the issue of place behind, and turn our focus to the props and performances involved in the rituals of magic production in contemporary spas.

In Mauss' thinking, magical rites are the fundamental corner-stones upon which magic is based. These rites are collective, taking an agreed form that is itself repetitively performed in much the same way, over and over again. As he pointed out, 'actions which are never repeated cannot be called magical. If the whole community does not believe in the efficacy of a group of actions, they cannot be magical. The form of the ritual is eminently transmissible and this is sanctioned by public opinion.' (Mauss 2001: 23) In this sense, magic is differ-ent from the private superstitions of an individual, because the rites through which it is produced take a collectively agreed upon form. They are social phenomena anchored in a culturally bound system of beliefs, and performed in specific places. They 'are eminently effective; they are creative; they do things' (ibid.). But in order to do things, they draw upon, and make use of other materials and substances 'that are not just everyday things' (2001: 58).

The rites of affectation performed in contemporary spas invoke an array of substances that are designed to mobilize external powers and transfer their regenerative potential into the body. Muds, for example, are spread out along the surfaces of bodies, and their different qualities are said to seep into the skin. Oils are used in a similar manner, and can even be coupled with the use of heating blankets that are said to further facilitate the ability of the oils' properties to penetrate the body. In other cases, rituals are designed to recharge bodies by setting them in motion through gymnastics and aerobic exercise, or alternatively by bringing them to a standstill in moments of meditation. And of course, all the while bodies are massaged, rubbed, touched, and stroked. As one spa manager explained: "We know that when you have a massage, many things happen in your body. Anti-stress hormones accumulate, knotted muscles loosen up, and blood circulation increases. Being touched is vitally important to us." The power of touch, in other words, is perhaps the most central force and tool of transformation at the disposal of spas.

The specialty at Varberg Kurort is the 'seaweed bath', which involves submersion in a special wooden tub to be scrubbed with seaweed by an assistant who monitors the temperature of the water, making sure it is neither too cold nor too warm. Following the seaweed scrub, the bather is left alone to float in the water, and listen to meditative music. Amongst well-initiated bathers there is an understanding that this is supposed to be a moment of relaxation. For the spa novice, however, the whole ritual can easily be laced with tensions of sexuality, or self-consciousness over the appearances of one's own body in the eyes of the strangers employed to pamper you. Involuntary but nonetheless haunting questions can spoil the moment: 'Should I take my shorts off?' 'Should I speak with the woman scrubbing me?' 'Will she be back to get me out of this tub, or am I supposed to leave when I get bored with the music?' 'Why didn't I loose a few pounds before coming here?' In this sense the magic of the moment can be extraordinarily fragile; the key to success lies in waking the

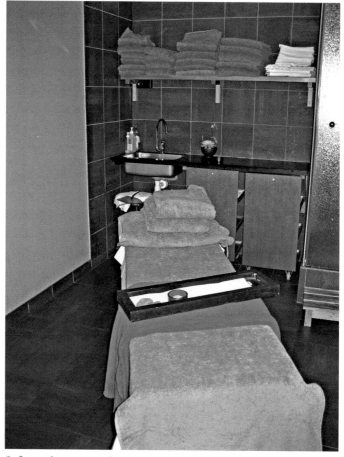

Soft towels are not only sources of comfort and warmth. They are also tools used by spa personnel in the course of a massage. They work to channel the energies of the spa, and to thereby help frame and control the expectations of the spa visitor. Photo: Tom O'Dell.

'right' types of energy, while allowing others to remain dormant. In the seaweed bath, cordial silence, a professionally unfocused and non-judgmental gaze, along with a handful of abrasive seaweed and decidedly firm (not-too-friendly) scrubbing, all work to keep everyone focused on the proper forms of energy.

Similar ritualized practices are of central importance in the massage-rooms. Here towels take on a special role. As the guest enters the massage-room, s/he is given instruction on how to lie on the massage table, and as the person in question removes her/his robe and approaches the table, it is not uncommon for the masseuse to unfold a large white cotton towel and hold it up above eye-level, where it acts like a screen shielding the disrobed body from the masseuse's gaze. After this, it is gently lowered onto the guest and straightened out. Once in place, it is folded back and forth across the body with smooth and controlled movements as the masseuse goes to work. Through this ritual of the fold, the body is opened to 'the power of touch' one segment at a time – the back, a leg, then the other leg, and so forth. In part, the folding and unfolding of the towel is akin to a dramatic production with the opening and closing of the stage curtain at the beginning and end of every act. Each fold signals a shift in attention, and a new moment of anticipation as a new portion of the body is exposed, and prepared for touching. And with each fold, another portion of the body is re-covered, enwrapped, and warmed by the soft cotton fibers of the towel – signaling the end of the act, and the commencement of a time of relaxation for that body part. This is the micro-drama of the fold.

But in addition to working as a dramatic device, the ritual of the fold can also be understood as a ritual of objectification that has parallels in the activities of a surgeon who only exposes that portion of the body that is to be operated on. The movement of the towel continuously frames and reframes the guest's body, symbolically transforming the guest from an individual in her/his entirety with desires and wants into series of parts – limbs, muscle groups, and surfaces – that are to be worked upon. And even as the textility of the towel intimately enwraps, comforts, and warms the body of the guest, it also separates the masseuse from that body, partially desexualizing the entire massage experience in the process. In this sense, the towel is not only an instrument of modesty, but also a vital tool in the spa's efforts to manage the 'right' types of energies.

That said, however, when it comes to energy management and the rites of affectation, water still remains the most important element at the disposal of spas, although the uses and beliefs tied to it have changed over time. While taking the waters was thought in past centuries to heal the body and cure a long list of ailments,

75

these supposed health benefits were largely dismissed by the end of the nineteenth century (Mansén 2001: 313ff). Nonetheless, small pockets of hope remained invested in the potential of water long into the twentieth century. Hydrology, for example, was one of the fastest growing medical fields in France in the early twentieth century, and although it became marginalized as a field of medical practice after the Second World War, it remained a required course of study in French medical schools until 1968 (Weisz 2001: 464 & 481). More popularly, the linkage between water and health received broader fortification in the 1990s as water once again came to be framed as a health drink, this time in the form of bottled water sold at high prices.

At approximately the same time, the belief in the curative potential of water enjoyed a renaissance of its own in the world of spas. This time, however, rather than focusing upon the chemical properties of the substance, or its 'medicinal power' to physically heal the sick, water came to be re-invoked in a growing number of spas through a series of ritualized uses intended to facilitate the sensation that one was in the midst of an inwardly focused 'recharging' process. Working towards these ends, spas have proven to be extremely creative in finding new uses for water. This is a world focused upon relaxation in which bodies are constantly submitted to heated pools, cold baths, steam-baths, bubble baths, salt-water pools (or natural ocean water), spring water, and arid saunas marked by the total absence of water. And all the while, visitors are still highly encouraged to indulge themselves through the actual drinking of water.

The explicit objective of all of this bathing, bubbling, and scrubbing is said to be the production of well-being that is achieved by the uniting of the senses, body, and soul.[12] But with such a diverse assortment of treatments available, there are evidently many routes to this end. Perhaps one of the most extreme ways in which this goal is striven after by some spas comes in the form of 'floating'. In a floating treatment the guest is enclosed in a shallow fiberglass tank filled a foot deep with a highly concentrated saline solution warmed to body temperature. Once in the tank, the lid is closed and the guest literally floats in total darkness, buoyed by the salt water. The confines of the tank make even the simplest of movements (such as the bending of the legs) difficult. In the tank, guests are not only brought to a standstill, but they are also completely cut off from the outside world and (ideally) their own senses. As one spa brochure explained, 'Experience weightlessness and silence in the floating tank's warm saltwater. When the body is not exposed to any form of outer influence – pressure, sound, light, or temperature – the body has the opportunity to "take care of itself".' (*Ystads Saltsjöbad* brochure 2005: 10)

On the surface of things, the floating tank would seem to be a highly rationalized and modern piece of technological equipment precariously located on the border between health and adventure. A vessel made of polished white fiberglass, featuring built-in lights that can be turned on from the inside should the darkness become overwhelming, it is filled with water whose temperature, quality, and saline content are carefully monitored and controlled with scientific methods. And indeed, within the spa industry the effects of the tank are described, on one level, in strictly medical terms, which refer to the effects of weightlessness upon the anatomy and musculature of the body. At the same time, part of the allure of the tank clearly comes from the space age experience of weightlessness it offers. The tank may have physiological effects upon the body, but it simultaneously offers guests, like many amusement park rides, a new experience: in this case, that of weightlessness and sensory deprivation. In this sense, part of the attraction of the tank is certainly facilitated by the manner in which it piques the imagination, stimulates the fantasy, and ultimately might simply prove to be 'good fun' – and these are all issues that shall be explored more fully in the next chapter. But beyond the medical terminology in which the spa industry embeds the floating experience, and the thrill of the new experience it may extend to potential guests, one even finds a more spiritual dimension working to give meaning to much of the floating experience. Once again, New Age philosophies play an important role in providing meaning to this experience. However, in order to more fully understand the manner in which New Age spirituality, well-being, and leisure practices are increasingly entwined in Swedish spas, we need to take a moment and look more closely at a few of the fundamental premises upon which New Age philosophies rest.

This is a subject that Paul Heelas has addressed extensively (see Heelas 1996, 1999 & 2002). As he points out, the New Age is a highly diverse phenomenon with many different and at times contradictory orientations. But there are, he argues, a few common denominators at the root of much of what is at issue here:

> The New Age is manifested when people realise or experience their true nature. The New Age teaches a highly optimistic – as spiritual – form of humanism. The self itself is to be celebrated. By nature we are perfect. To experience the Self itself – within the person as well as within the natural order as a whole – is to experience 'God', the 'Goddess', the 'source', the 'inner child', 'Christ consciousness', 'truth', or simply 'inner spirituality'. (1999: 52)

Unfortunately, contact with this 'inner spirituality' is disrupted and made imperfect by much of modern life, including the pursuit for material things. And here the ultimate objective of the New Age is to help the individual find her/his way back to the true Self, or as Heelas phrases it, 'To go within' (ibid.).

In the dark confines of the floating tank, self-imposed sensory deprivation is intended (and said) to work along these lines, offering the ultimate opportunity for bodies to relax and 'care for themselves' – providing the user with a sensation that some spa patrons I have encountered describe as 'simply wonderful'. The tank does this by separating the individual, physically and sensually, from the outside world. In so doing, it also separates the body from all the contaminative stimuli to which it is exposed over the course of daily life. These are stimuli which the rhetoric of spas argues – echoing New Age tenets concerning the contaminative effects of daily life upon our inner being – run interference patterns on our bodies. The power of the floating tank thus derives largely from the ability it is said to have in providing the body with a space in which it can reconnect to itself, heal itself, and more effectively recharge itself. As Hasseludden's promotional material explains, 'The treatment [45 minutes in length] corresponds to approximately six hours of sleep in terms of recovery for the body'.[13] In this sense, the floating tank can be understood as a time-machine of sorts, capable of compressing several hours of regeneration and rest into less than a single hour, but it is also a *sanctum sanctorum* for the body and soul – a space of purification in which body and soul can once again reconnect, allowing the powers of healing to come from within.

However, it is important to bear in mind that belief in the healing effects of the floating tanks is also simultaneously anchored in a more medically and scientifically oriented discourse in which people speak of knotted muscles, cramps, and the manner in which floating can facilitate forms of relaxation that diminish these problems. As Hasseludden's promotional material argues, 'Research has shown that floating increases blood circulation and strengthens the immune system. The brain produces theta waves, which are active in the type of deep relaxation in a woken state that is achieved after long training in meditation.'[14] Rather than contradicting the streams of New Age philosophy noted above, the medicinal discourse of healing works parallel to them, providing a medical vocabulary with which to discuss the process of healing from within.

Echoing this tendency, one spa manager I spoke with passionately described the effects a floating session could have on whiplash victims, and with a great deal of enthusiasm described his hopes of being able to work together with the local health authorities to develop the medical applications of this technology for such victims. In nearly the same breath, however, he also urged me to try a floating session using a less than scientific appeal:

> You have to do it. You really do! Because what happens when you're lying in the tank and really *let your body take over* … you relax. And if you fall asleep you almost come into some form of deep sleep so that you feel like you've rested. You haven't just rested your muscles and body, but also your brain. [My emphasis]

He did not explicitly mention the effects of the tank upon the soul or the inner Self, but emphasized the potential of the tank to have a transformational effect upon me – an effect that would allow my 'body take over' and that could result in a special form of sleep, providing rest to not only the body and muscles, but even more deeply, to my brain. In print, his words might seem strikingly close to a sales pitch, but they were spoken in earnest and with conviction, stemming from his own experiences. As proof of his sincerity, he booked me for a full floating session, at his expense – and as it turned out, I learned that attaining relaxation via floating involved much more than simply floating in a tank of salt water.

Floating rites

In considering the experience of the floating tank, it is helpful to compare it with the technology of the solarium, as such a comparison helps to highlight the importance that ritual performance plays in framing and providing special meaning to the spa experience. Superficially, solariums and floating tanks show many similarities. Both are machines that are designed to have an effect upon the human body. In both the user enters the machine, lies down, and closes the lid for a specified period of time. Beyond this point, however, the machines differ vastly in focus. While the solarium is intended to affect the outer surface of the body, 'tanning' it, the floating tank is expected to have an inner effect upon the body – having a calming and relaxing effect upon it. The tank is in essence a cathedral for the Self: a sacred realm distanced from the bustle of the profane world of everyday life. Stepping into the tank is in this sense a transitional movement between the realms of the profane and the sacred. But this is not a movement that is taken lightly; on the contrary, it is controlled and carefully orchestrated. Consequently, guests are not just given access to the floating tank, as is customarily the case with the solarium; they are led to it and instructed on the proper procedures for its effective use. Let me illustrate the manner in which this is handled with the floating session I was offered by the spa manager mentioned above.

Having arrived at the designated time for the floating session, an attendant guided me into a small room containing the tank, a shower, a small stereo on a shelf, and a lit candle. She explained, speaking slowly and softly, that after she left the room, I should get undressed and bathe naked in order to really feel the full effect of weightlessness. Before entering the tank, however, I should check over my entire body and cover any sores that I may have with vaseline, otherwise the salt water would sting. Having said this, she handed me a container of vaseline, a wooden tongue-depressor, and a paper cup. Her movements were slow and deliberate, reinforcing the perception that the room was isolated and separated from the normal pace of daily life. And I learned that the use of the vaseline involved a specific routine of its own. First, I was told, I should place a dab of vaseline in the cup, and use this to cover my sores. Once this procedure was completed, I could climb into the tank. But once again, I learned that there was another set of routines to follow before I could actually start to float. There was a light-switch at the back which I was told I should turn on prior to closing the lid. Once the lid was closed, I should place a small inflatable neck support under my head to keep it afloat. It was then appropriate to turn out the light and just float in darkness, trying to relax and think of nothing. If I fell asleep, and apparently many people did, I was not to worry because the attendant would keep track of time on my behalf and knock on the lid to get me out after 45 minutes.

Exiting the tank involved another established set of procedures. Opening the lid to the tank, I exited one world of darkness to enter another one, glowing in candlelight. From here I had been instructed to proceed with a warm shower to rinse the salt off my body. In the shower, a specially chosen cosmetic soap waited at my disposal, and next to the shower a large, soft, folded towel had been lain out for me. From there I was told to redress, and proceed out to the spa lounge which was fully lit. As I exited the room the attendant walked up to me slowly and asked if I enjoyed the treatment, and as she did this, she led me to a lounge with a fireplace and small fruit buffet. "Now sit down and just relax for a while here." She walked away, and the treatment was over.

Writing about transitional acts and everyday life in modern society, Christena Nippert-Eng argues for the need to appreciate the degree to which 'rituals help us make the transformations between everyday, profane selves and their special, sacred counterparts' (1995: 146). In the case of spas, it is impossible to understand the manner in which well-being and serenity are produced without an appreciation of the ritualistic aspects of the activities taking place within them. The rituals of the floating tank, like most of the rituals of the spa, are subtle, but crucial to its functioning. Step by step, with the aid of an attendant, the guest is led further and further away from the profane world – from the fully lit spa, to the candlelit floating room, to the darkness of the tank; from the tempo of the car ride to the spa, to the deliberately subdued gestures of the attendant, to the total stillness of the tank; from the connected social world of cell phones, to the corporeally oriented search for sores and use of vaseline, to the introspective and drowsy world of the tank. My point is that people do not just relax at spas, they are ritualistically led to relaxation and well-being. And this process of transformation is done step by step, fold by fold, and caress by caress. Time and time again. But where Nippert-Eng, drawing upon Durkheim's work with rituals (2001), argued for an understanding of rituals as a means of navigating between that which was sacred and that which was profane, I would argue that spa rituals, while framing the spa experience as special, also continuously allow for the blurring of the border between the sacred and the profane. This is a world in which physical and spiritual healing continuously co-exist alongside both new and traditional forms of pampering (including champagne lunches and classical massages), and in which the adventure of trying and experiencing something new is ever a part of the allure of the spa's services.

But in order to work in this way, the entire experience has to be carefully framed in advance. Guests, after all, do not come to spas as blank pages, they come full of expectations, and the representational work of the spa plays a central role in shaping and informing these expectations. Bearing this in mind, let us turn to the representational world of the spa.

Magical representations

The brochures and promotional materials used by Swedish spas set out to define the spa experience and to reinforce a collective focus upon the 'right' types of energies. For example, the 2002 brochure for Varberg features very little text but page after page of pictures, many of which depict empty rooms and inanimate objects aesthetically presented to create an appearance of calm: a pair of rubber boots and a rain hat on the beach; a woman's bathing suit drying in the breeze at the sea's edge; a bottle with a message in it. Symbolically, the brochure assures the reader that this is an uncluttered place in which even the most trivial details can come into focus, and the absence of people implicitly communicates the absence of bustle, worry, and stress. Where people are depicted, they are usually either alone or in heterosexual pairs: a young man in a suit lying against a tree in the forest; a woman contemplatively feeling the seawater with her hand; a young man and woman sitting by the sea's edge staring quietly into the distance. With a few exceptions the pictures show little sign of any form of communication between people. This is a world in which people predominantly seem to move about alone or silently in pairs.

A sense of stillness and separation from the outside world is further reinforced by the manner in which bodies are visually dissected into separated and unconnected parts: objectified and totally removed from the context of the larger daily life they would otherwise be incorporated into. Here we see a head wrapped in a towel, partially hidden by a white face pack; a foot on the edge of a tub with seaweed hanging between the toes; a man's head and upper chest emerging out of a completely still sea. Occasionally, there is even a pair of hands touching or caressing the person who is the subject of the photograph. Usually these hands are physically holding, or pressing down (in a massage-like motion) upon the person in the picture. In both cases they emphasize the slowness of the experience, and the fact that you will be cared for. But they are even images of restraint – if the tempo of society seems to be speeding up, the spa employs people who will hold you in place, and physically force you to slow down.

Hasseludden's promotional materials invoke a nearly identical symbolic grammar. Here we find pictures of single objects (a towel by the pool, a bucket containing a crumpled Japanese robe), partial bodies (a portion of a man's face shown being massaged, a woman's back being massaged), and single people or heterosexual pairs (a woman's head sticking out of a pool of water, a man and woman in a steamy pool). Reflecting one of the facility's more important markets (that of conferences), Hasseludden's promotional material focuses marginally more on groups of people interacting than does Varberg Kurort's brochure, but other than this, the largest difference is simply Hasseludden's focus upon its Japanese theme, while Varberg aligns itself more closely with the Swedish nature surrounding the spa.

Both Varberg and Hasseludden reinforce the image that they are places capable of working magic by lacing the presentation of their spaces with a degree of spirituality. They do this, however, in slightly different ways. For Varberg, the key comes in the simple form of sunlight. As Richard Dyer has pointed out, since the Middle Ages, art in the Christian world has used the representation of light from above, especially sunlight, to depict the flow of power from above. This has been portrayed in many indirect ways over the centuries, from the appearance of halos in medieval paintings to the use of halo effects in modern popular films. However, it has even been continuously invoked directly though the image of sunlight streaming down upon particular individuals and icons. Pointing to this rooting in Christian ideology, Dyer lucidly argues that:

> The culture of light makes seeing by means and in terms of light central to the construction of the human image ... Those who can let the light through, however, dividedly, with however much struggle, those whose bodies are touched by the light from above, who yearn upwards towards it, those are the people who should rule and inherit the earth. (Dyer 1997: 121)

Viewing the Varberg brochure against this background, we find an iconographic linkage to Christianity and an implicitly understood signification of privileged position that thoroughly permeates the brochure. The woman touching the sea that I mentioned above is lit from above and to the left by what appears to be a fading sunlight. On the same page to the left of her is a picture of the sun setting over the sea. On the preceding two pages the same woman leans against the side of an indoor pool with her eyes closed, and her head resting on her hands – and she is bathed in sunlight. In a picture above her, a young man in a bathing suit sits on the floor in the sun in the same pool room with his eyes closed and head lifted toward the sun. The pattern continuously repeats itself.

In part, it might be argued that the pictures evoke a sense of warmth. In Scandinavia, with its long dark winters, the sun also serves as a symbol of hope, freedom, and better times. All of this also plays into the brochure. However, the sun in the Varberg brochure isolates the subjects of the photographs. They do not just happen to be in the sun, they seem to consume it, as though this were a central source of their rejuvenation.[15]

The realm of the holy is invoked in a very different way by Hasseludden's promotional material. While the sacral content of Varberg's brochure is largely expressed on the symbolic plane of visual representation, Hasseludden is more explicit in framing its services with their intangible effects upon the 'soul'. And they go so far as to claim that they offer 'massage methods in which the body and soul are treated simultaneously'[16]. Beyond this, the Japanese theme of the spa itself has linkages to the spiritual. Theirs is not a high tech, modern Japan, but one located in a mythical past of robes, traditions, and ceremonies. It is the Other, located in another time gone by (or rapidly fading time) in which it seems only natural to find (and depict) people in meditative prayer. This is a juncture at which orientalism nourishes New Age beliefs focused upon the self, such as their claim that their Shiatsu massage can 'invigorate the body's flow of energy … It works to open your energy paths so that the energy can flow freely. Even if Shiatsu is an energy-bestowing massage, you will feel serene and in harmony when it is over.'[17]

At Hasseludden the invocation of New Age imagery and ideas is a carefully weighed strategy used by management. Underlining this, one of the managers at Hasseludden specifically identified what he called 'commercialized spiritual care' as a potential up-and-coming commodity, and he even framed Hasseludden's flirtation with New Age philosophies as a step in this direction. In positioning itself in this way, Hasseludden has in essence consciously aligned itself with a growing international trend in which spas promote themselves by liberally invoking references to phenomena ranging from 'native healing traditions' to 'magical clay'.[18] Some spas, such as the Golden Door Spa in Arizona, even go as far as employing shamans to help care for their patrons (Zernike 2005: 9). And while the employment of shamans might sound like a somewhat radical move

The Japanese theme at Hasseludden invokes a mythical past of robes, traditions, and ceremonies that are reinforced by architectural cues that hark back to a world of temples and shrines from another era. Photo: Tom O'Dell.

in producing well-being, the use of spiritual expertise is not at all a foreign thought to the management of Hasseludden. As one of their brochures explains, 'In order to create a harmonious wholeness in which energies flow in the right way, we have received advice from a Feng-Shui master' (Yasuragi brochure *Sinnesro*, undated: 5).

But Hasseludden is not alone in making use of Eastern and New Age influences, and incorporating them into its list of offerings. As it turns out, meditation, Do-In, Qi Gong, 'The Tibetan Five', Tai Chi, and yoga are not just superficial accoutrements to the spa visit, nor are they mere representational tropes symbolizing relaxation. They are activities which a growing number of people seek out and which spas – even the most medically oriented of them, such as Varberg Kurort[19] – increasingly feel obliged to include amongst their offerings. As such, these activities are an indicator of the degree to

A sign at Hasseludden instructing visitors to 'Please be quiet. Meditation is being practiced'. Photo: Tom O'Dell.

which New Age beliefs are increasingly spreading through society and often surfacing in unexpected places.

Invocations of spirituality in spas are, in short, not 'just' vaguely alluded to through the ritual activities and representation in which spa treatments are embedded; they are increasingly of central importance to these spas. However, their importance cannot solely be explained in terms of the spread of New Age philosophies, or the spiritual 'Easternization' of the West (Campbell 1999). The aura of spirituality which is part of a spa visit, including the symbolic invocation of images inspired by centuries of Christian iconography, are also important cultural mechanisms that help spa visitors legitimize the pampering and enjoyment they receive at the spa. As one of the spa managers I interviewed pointed out, it is important for many of his customers to feel as though they have earned the right to be taken care of for a short time. The visit to the spa is framed as a treat for past sacrifices (cf. Miller 1998a: 40 ff.), but it is equally important that it not be perceived as an all too luxurious activity that needs to be defended and explained in the face of family, friends, and neighbors. Invocations of spirituality help to contain this threat by denying the spa visit too hedonistic an appearance, while helping to lend credibility to the claim that new energies and powers can be found and stored thanks to a spa visit.

The magical representations discussed here may primarily be linked to a limited number of specific spas with slightly different profiles; however, the symbols they choose to invoke and the manner in which they do so are not at all unique to them. After all, other spas throughout the world work in very similar ways; magazines ranging from *Time, Better Homes and Gardens*, and *The Luxury Spa Finder* to a whole slew of magazines dedicated to questions of interior design and modern living are part of the spell-casting machinery that pumps out advertisements and special issues bearing similar images and descriptions of the latest trends and opportunities in the world of spas. Thus when one Swedish magazine rhetorically asked its readers, 'So what do you say about starting to collect grandiose experiences intended to counteract the wear and tear done to the body and soul?' (Swanberg 2001: 113), not only was a resounding 'Yes!' the anticipated answer, but readers were even expected to understand that these types of experiences could be regarded as collectables, capable of being conjured forth time and time again – given the appropriate conditions. By the early years of the new millenium, serenity, in other words, was well on its way to becoming a mass-produced and industrialized commodity.

But is it really magic?

> Magic gives form and shape to those poorly coordinated or impo-
> tent gestures by which the needs of the individual are expressed,
> and because it does this through ritual, it renders them effective
> (Mauss 2001: 175).

In trying to capture and explain the essence of magic, Marcel Mauss concluded that magic was nothing if it were not a social phenomenon (2001: 174). Spas such as Varberg Kurort, Varberg's Asia Spa, and Hasseludden go to great lengths to help their patrons feel as though they have entered a blank space detached from the problems of the surrounding world. However, their rise in popularity over the past decade curiously coincides with the neo-liberalism that has washed over much of Europe and North America. They have grown in strength at the same time as the welfare state, with its protective and paternalistic social policies, has been put on the retreat. Where citizens once expected to receive support from larger collectives, they are now increasingly left with the responsibility of taking care of themselves.[20]

Spa patrons are a heterogeneous group of consumers whose motivations for going to a spa are nearly as diverse as the patrons themselves. To be sure, amongst the people who have shared their experiences with me, visits to spas are often described as cozy, lovely, and luxurious; they are understood to constitute a golden opportunity to spoil oneself a little bit. In other words, the visits are undertaken because they perceive them to be fun, but in contrast to many other types of leisure activities, spa visits are also often framed as something more than just a light form of leisure. They are an indulgence which has been earned through hard work, but to this end, they are also often described as a counter to the demands, uncertainties, and stresses of working life, and in this sense they are a highly ritualized form of 'serious play' (Schrage 1999) in which having fun is at times framed as a path to increased (or continued) professional productivity.

Echoing this perspective, spa managers themselves also see a clear linkage between the growing market for well-being, widespread concerns over burn-out, and associated perceptions that working life is becoming increasingly stressful.[21] As one manager explained,

> As we see things, there is a very clear connection, and we don't have anything against that connection I should add … because whether you like it or not, I think the future for those who work, the content of their work is going to be demanding. It's going to be tough. Working days will be tough, and the demands placed upon employees are not going to diminish. People are going to have to find some kind of balance in all of this.

89

And another manager, reflecting upon the fact that the time between the date a conference (or private) booking is made and the date of the actual visit is becoming ever shorter, remarked, 'I think it's the tough pace of life in society today. In the workplace people suddenly realize, "No, we have to get away with everyone in the company. Off to a conference!"' Behind the magic, the managers of spas are aware that they are encountering a form of concern and uncertainty, as individuals as well as entire places of work fear that they are about to come apart at the seams. The spa is here not only a place in which to recharge batteries, for some it is also a last resort.

Within this context, it is perhaps not surprising to find that people's anxieties have led to the development of 'new' arenas in which they hope to find a hospitable space capable of providing them with a temporary haven from stress, a potential source of rejuvenation. The commercialized hospitality of the spa may be a far cry from any form of pure hospitality in Derrida's sense, but for Swedish patrons it seems to be developing into a surrogate sanctuary in which they increasingly place their hopes and experiment with new forms of spirituality, even as this occurs in the name of fun and relaxation.

In this regard, spas offer an oasis in which those with the means can search for a quick fix of energy. The degree to which spas can actually provide this sensation varies from case to case. Nonetheless, whether one speaks with managers, masseuses, or the patrons they serve, there is a widespread belief in the power of the touch, and in the fact that a stay at a spa can help people feel better. In the cases where patrons do leave the spa feeling better, I would argue that magic has been worked. It is a magic that stems from both a will to believe and an actual belief.[22] However, it is also a magic that is embedded in a larger cultural context that, as I have argued, supports these systems of beliefs. The effects of this particular form of magic are most easily accessible to the affluent (magic has all too often proven to be an expensive commodity demanding sacrifices of its own), but the desire to partake of magic can clearly be found through all levels of society – expressed most clearly in the ever-growing supply of products and magazine articles that help people make their own spas inexpensively at home (a phenomenon addressed more fully in chapter five).

Noting the growing role fantasies play as an aspect of daily life, Žižek has argued that 'fantasy constitutes our desire, provides its co-ordinates; that is, it literally "teaches us how to desire".' (Žižek 1997: 7) The fantasy about the well of eternal youth that spas draw so heavily upon is arguably one of humanity's oldest fantasies, and is itself linked to the desire to live and achieve just a little bit more. In an age in which we are all increasingly expected to fend for ourselves, it is perhaps not surprising to find that our anxieties and desires have led to the development of 'new' arenas – such as spas – in which individuals hope to find a small advantage that they can use against their competitors (that is, everyone else).

Whether or not any of that which has been described in this chapter is actually magical can perhaps be debated, but the material presented here points to a need to understand better the manner in which spirituality and leisure are entwined in economic and cultural processes that are only partially visible at first glance. Of all social scientists, Durkheim has done the most to set the tone of the argument for the need to understand the realms of the profane and sacral as distinctly different and separate (2001: 36ff). But in the world of spas – whether we are discussing the architectural and material organization of the facilities themselves, the rituals of towel folding, or the technologies of floating – it is interesting to note how the sacred and profane continuously telescope into each other, making the border between them diffuse at times. A visit to a spa may be seen as a way of pampering or spoiling oneself, and of having fun, but in order to work, it is dependent upon a densely woven web of rituals, props, and representations that provide the spa visit with its cultural energy, and move it that much closer to being a magical experience of sorts – and if nothing else, a homage to the Self.

Whereas the Swedish spas of the nineteenth century derived much of their popularity from the social and collective forms of activities they could extend to their patrons, the hospitality of spas today has been honed to facilitate the creation of specific forms of disjuncture and isolation as patrons remove themselves from society to get in touch with themselves. Along the way, and in conjunction with this, the curative practices of these facilities have shifted from the healing of physical ailments to an increasing attention on the alleviation of spiritual rupture. But as the next chapter illustrates, spas do more than produce disjuncture in the name of well-being. They also bring some people together, while binding others more tightly to the stresses of working life.

In order to more clearly examine how this works, the following chapter shall more closely analyze the cultural organization of the body and the senses at spas, and the manner in which they interact with the material environment of the facilities in question here. Along the way, while still focusing upon the body and physical routines of the spa, the chapter will also focus upon the personnel of the spa (the magicians if you will) and their work.

CHAPTER 4

Spa Sensibilities

Repetitious spaces are the outcome of repetitive gestures (those of the workers) … Are these spaces interchangeable because they are homologous? Or are they homogeneous so that they can be exchanged, bought and sold, with the only differences between them being those assessable in money?   (Lefebvre, 1991: 75)

Take a few deep breaths, unwind, relax – now it's your time.
(*Varberg's Kurort Hotel & Spa* brochure, undated[1])

When you're standing there by the reception and they come and get you for your treatment … the woman who was going to take care of me kind of held me the entire time. She held me around the shoulders and led me to the treatment room. Very caringly, it was. So it was actually very comforting. I felt, 'Yeah, they're going to take care of me'.

(An informant describing the moments
leading up to her treatment.)

The enchanting rituals of the spa and the repetitive actions performed by their personnel are important avenues through which spas are capable of delivering the sensation of well-being to their guests. But clearly, there is more to spas than can be explained simply by references to the realm of the mystical. Spas might promote themselves by promising very abstract and intangible products, from harmony and balance to reinvigoration and free-flowing energy – and the people with whom I have spoken who attend spas claim to be looking for these same qualities, as well as a sense of coziness, luxury, and pampering – but in practice spas are very physically oriented places whose activities are directed towards the body and senses of their patrons.

It is the body and senses which are stimulated and manipulated in the pursuit of wellness, yet it might be argued that in the world of spas, the body and senses are as much a means to an end of the spas' activities as the end itself; biological healing may be one of the outcomes of a spa visit, but equally (or perhaps more) important is the emotional impact a visit has upon patrons. Where eighteenth- and nineteenth-century guests came to cure physical ailments ranging from gout to paralysis, their present-day peers are more often than not hoping to find emotional transformation and the establishment of new states of mind. Serenity, enjoyment, calm, entitlement, a sense of 'being at one with oneself', or of being spoiled and taken care of, these are all part of the affective parameters that are expected of a spa visit. But in order to reach the realm of affect, spas have to work through the bodies and senses of their patrons.[2]

The following chapter focuses upon a cultural analysis of the manner in which this works. In order to do this, the chapter begins by problematizing the concept of affect and the manner in which it can be understood as a culturally and socially organized phenomenon. It then proceeds by examining the way in which contemporary Swedish spas actually organize themselves materially and spatially to impress themselves upon the bodies, senses, and emotions of their guests. While the rituals and representational work which spas engage in (and which were the subject of the previous chapter) are highly important in framing the spa experience, this chapter pushes the line of analysis one step further, arguing for a need to understand the manner in which emotions, as they find expression in such feelings as well-being or stress, may be linked to rhythms of movement taking place in spas as bodies interact with the material world around them. As part of the line of argumentation presented below, the chapter will challenge Cartesian-inspired understandings of the division between mind and body, arguing instead for a need to better comprehend the ways in which embodied perceptions of the world around us take form and find expression through the body and senses as well as the mind.

Emotion, culture, and corporeality

Rather than modelling people as either thinking *or* feeling, we might view people as almost always 'emotional' in the sense of being committed to 'processing information' or understanding the

world in certain culturally and personally constructed ways. (Lutz
1998: 225, emphasis in the original)

Affect is something of a strange subject. On the one hand, there exists
a great deal of uncertainty as to how we can understand affect from a
cultural perspective, but on the other hand, emotions are phenomena
that everyone is intimately familiar with. We live with our emotions
and relate to the world through them. In a world in which everything
is for sale and seemingly attainable in commodity form, from the most
trivial items we use in daily life such as soap and toilet paper to the
most exotic experience of another culture or spiritual enlightenment,
our emotions seem to be the last bastion of authenticity. 'What I feel',
our common sense tells us, 'has to be the greatest testament of who I
really am, because my feelings come from within me.' Understood in
this way, affect is a very personal experience bound to the individual,
uniquely connected to the self, and encompassed by it.

This sort of common-sense perception of emotions as internally
produced phenomena has a great deal of scholarly and theoretical
support of its own. Since the mid-nineteenth century much of psy-
chiatry has worked to reinforce this perspective. Searching for the
roots of such affective disorders as hysteria, weak nerves, anxiety, and
fugue states, psychiatrists opened a whole field of research dedicated
to the dissection, labeling and examination of the inner workings of
the psyche (cf. Foucault 1978; Hacking 1998). And while aspects
of this research have been called into question by contemporary
scholars, my intention here is not to deny the existence of a linkage
between biology and emotion. Serotonin, dopamine, hormones,
endorphins, neurotransmitters – they all exist and play a role in the
formation of emotions (see Damasio 2003: 60 ff.).

However, over the course of the past few decades a growing body
of research has increasingly drawn attention to the fact that emotions
are much more than biological phenomena. They have social and
cultural roots which seem to be of at least as much importance in
the framing and production of affect as any biological linkages (Lutz
1998: 5). As Arlie Russell Hochschild reminds us, 'emotions always
involve the body, but they are not sealed biological events' (2003:
125). Consequently, laughter has a tendency to be projected upwards

in social hierarchies, as people are more likely to laugh (longer and harder) at the jokes of their superiors than those of their subordinates. By contrast, anger and frustration have trajectories that take them more frequently down social hierarchies, as these emotions are directed at subordinates (Hochschild 2003). The formation of our emotions is thus influenced by the nature of our encounters with other people, and the types of social relations in which those encounters are enmeshed. Social structures of power are one point of cultural inflection through which emotions develop, but anyone who has attended a wedding, funeral, or public sporting event can attest to the significance the presence of others plays in the constitution of an emotional atmosphere. It is one thing to watch a wedding video or sports match on television, but quite another thing to participate in the actual event with other people.

Once again, this may seem like common sense, but a realization of the fact that affect is more than an isolated biological event raises a number of questions. Issues of sociality may be important, but central here are questions concerning the relationship between the body, senses, and outside world. In part it can be argued that it is through our senses that we come to understand the world around us and relate to it. It might be the *sight* of a child laughing and playing that fills us with happiness, the *smell* of home-made cooking which envelopes us with a sense of comfort or warmth, the *sound* of a back-firing car that fills a war veteran with instant terror, or the prickly *feeling* of a pair of woolen pants that re-awakens childhood angst. Thus the world around us reaches into us and proceeds to impress itself upon us (materially, spatially, and sensually), but this is not a simple one-way process.

As we come to know the world through corporeal impressions of it, we are consciously and unconsciously orienting ourselves toward it, anticipating it, and giving it form (cf. Damasio 2003). Viewed in this way, scholars are increasingly becoming aware that affect is more than a biological event or consequence of outside stimuli. It is a corporeally anchored way of knowing the world, and in this sense it can be understood, as Nigel Thrift has argued, as '*a form of thinking,* often indirect and non-reflective, it is true, but thinking all the same' (2004: 60). As we go through daily life, feeling that certain situations are stressful, relaxing, enjoyable, and so on, we are simultaneously engaging in an intuitive process in which we are preparing to respond to coming events as they unfold. Our brain filters through the information it is bombarded with as part of the process of making sense out of the surrounding world and cultur- ally organizing it. But as Tor Nørretranders has demonstrated in his studies of the formation of consciousness, this is a process that takes time. The average person needs between 0.8 and 1.5 seconds to become conscious of ongoing events (Nørretranders 1998: 215). Consciousness is, consequently, always an after-the-fact construction. However, the body and senses work in present-time – informed in the first instance not necessarily by a conscious awareness of the present, but the processes of affect in which the body is enmeshed as it kinesthetically engages the world around it (Lakoff & Johnson 1999: 4 ff.). And it is against this background, drawing upon the work of cognitive scientists and philosophers, that Thrift has argued for a greater recognition of the manner in which 'body practices rely on the emotions as a crucial element of the body's apprehension of the world; emotions are a vital part of the body's anticipation of the moment' (2004: 67). In anticipating the world through our emotions, we begin to give it shape even before we are conscious of it. Thus, affect is not solely an outcome of our interaction with the world, but should even be understood as a form of embodied knowledge giving shape to the world.

In order to deliver upon the promises they make, spas thus have to carefully work, shape, and control a space of anticipation in the pre-reflexive gap between their clients' bodies and senses, and their reflective awareness of the events unfolding around them. Emotional management requires an astute attention to the details of the mate- rial organization of the spa and the kinesthetic rhythms of those moving around within their confines. As a means of laying out the implications of this discussion, I wish to return to Hasseludden and Varberg Kurort to analyze the manner in which bodies, emotions, and materiality are interwoven in the spatial confines of Swedish spas. Later in the chapter I will introduce material from another spa, Scania Spa by the Sea, located in the south of Sweden.[3] But for now, let us begin with Varberg's lobby.

Material culture and sensual communication

The bandwidth of language is far lower than the bandwidth of sensation. Most of what we know about the world we can never tell each other (Nørretranders, 1998: 309).

As one of the managers at Varberg Kurort explained in the previous chapter, the lobby at Varberg Kurort seems to have the ability to instill a sense of serenity upon visitors. While there is a symbolic and representational explanation for this, beyond it is a corporeal explanation that needs to be examined. As people enter the lobby in the morning, they not only move into a room that is darker than the outside surroundings, but they actually enter an institutional environment (that of a previous sanatorium). Loud voices and noises produce echoes that, like ghosts, bounce off the walls and hard floors, and come back to haunt all within the lobby. This leads not only to the dampening of voices, but even (at least for some) to diminished and more constrained gestures and softer footsteps, which in turn lead to slower and shorter strides. In this sense, synaesthesia, 'the transposition of sensory images or sensory attributes from one modality to another' (Marks 1978: 8, quoted in Feld, 2005: 181; see also Howe 2005a: 292; and O'Dell 2005c), is an important catalyst in the production of a 'sense of serenity' in the Varberg lobby that implicates the collusive interaction of the eyes and ears upon the unsuspecting musculature of the body.

The Japanese theme at Hasseludden also works the senses of its visitors, but in a rather different manner. The sparsely decorated interior plays upon the notion of stripping away all that is excessive, of returning to a purer aesthetic and spiritual state. This aesthetic state is itself transferred into the bodies of visitors, at least in part, with the aid of the *yukata* robes that guests are asked to wear. As one of the managers of Hasseludden explained to me, the *yukata* sits tight around the body and inhibits movement. It is, in other words, physically constraining, and forces visitors into a new, slower rhythm of movement, which is then further accentuated by thin, light, cotton slippers which guests are provided with along with their *yukata* and are encouraged to wear. The slippers do not sit well on the foot, and have a tendency to glide off as you walk. They are also very slippery on the sleek wooden and stone floors of Hasseludden, providing a sensation akin to ice-skating in untied skates. The combined result of the *yukata* and slippers is a radically altered kinesthetic condition, provoking not only new schemata of movement (shorter steps, shuffling feet, the working of the toes to keep the slippers on), but also a new form and focus of concentration (and consciousness) upon bodily tempo, tactility, and coordination.[4]

However, the efforts of spas to reach into and affect bodies do not stop there. Massage and treatment rooms are also carefully arranged and organized. As part of this, different colors are used in the interiors of these rooms in order to evoke different moods. At Varberg, for example, the spa management explained that they periodically change the color schemes of the waiting-rooms for the seaweed baths, in the hope that this will provide returning guests with the sensation of having experienced something new. In the world of hotels, rooms are continuously refurbished as they age and become worn refurbishment maintains a certain standard of convenience. In contrast, the logic driving the refurbishment of the seaweed bath waiting-rooms is more explicitly driven by a desire to reach into the bather's being and have an emotive effect upon him or her.

In this sense the boundaries of rooms are delineated not only by doors, walls, and windows, but also by divergent atmospheres of sensory stimulation. Rooms containing indoor pools, for example, feel humid, smell of chlorine, and possess a unique reverberative sound quality that is very different from a carpeted hotel corridor. Similar principles work as one moves from room to room in a spa. One area may smell of fresh flowers, while another carries the lingering scent of disinfectant, and a third is marked by a new and strange odor that may be an aloe vera oil, a body lotion, or burning incense. The result is that as visitors dampen their voices and physically slow down, their olfactory senses are constantly triggered and spurred to new states of arousal.

In a similar manner, music is used to furnish treatment rooms, providing each room with a unique soundscape. To this end, New Age, oriental, or classical music, as well as sedate forms of modern pop, are utilized to create what Jo Tacchi has likened to an auditory 'texture' (1998: 26) in the spa experience. But the rhythms of the

At Hasseludden a Feng-Shui master has been called upon to help the spa produce the right atmosphere for relaxation. The sparsely decorated interior of the spa plays upon the notion of stripping away all that is excessive, of returning to a purer aesthetic and spiritual state. Photo: Tom O'Dell.

music that accompany a treatment do more than just provide the experience with a further texture. Sound leaves traces; it moves, and is consequently marked by a time of its own (Feld, 2005: 185). Doppler effects, for example, mark comings and goings, indicating the future, present, and history of sound through shifts in pitch. Footsteps fade as others walk away from us. In the massage-room, New Age music may be played in the hope that it will have a calming effect; however, part of this effect is derived from the fact that the music does not actually move anywhere in relation to the person being massaged. In a world in which we are (unconsciously) used to the fact that sounds circulate and move, stasis and immobility are further accentuated by the experience of 'audio immobility' that lasts the duration of the massage or treatment at the spa. In a sense, audio time does actually stand still here.[5]

Beyond the treatment rooms, water provides a prevalent if understated aural backdrop to the spa experience. It laps at the sides of pools, splashes with the movement of bodies in those pools, drops

The atmosphere created around Hasseludden's indoor pool is in part a consequence of the visual aesthetic in which it is packed. But beyond this, the experience of the room is also derived from the acoustic and olfactory impact the room has upon the guest. Photo: Tom O'Dell.

off bodies and swimming apparel onto stone or tiled floors as people exit pools, and continuously bubbles and gurgles in the jacuzzi. In some pools, water flows continuously from specially designed faucets called 'cobras' (the name derives from their designed appearance which resembles that of a cobra). The intention is for these to be used by bathers as a massage source – by standing under the steady stream of water, bathers can subject their backs, necks or arms to the force of the water – but this flowing water also provides a steady aural stimulus that enwraps the soundscape of the pool area like a blanket.

These aquatic sounds are, for the most part, soft, rhythmic, and repetitive in nature. And as Veronica Strang has pointed out, this aural quality of water provides it with a calming quality of its own (2004: 52). But as she also points out, water also mesmerizes through its ability to reflect light and function almost as a light source. The light it casts is ever-moving, rhythmically swaying, flickering. 'It is not possible to do more than speculate about the effects of visual images that resonate with unconscious processes, but the ethnographic evidence is suggestive. It seems that, like the hypnotist's flickering candle or swirling optical images, the visual qualities of water are indeed mesmerizing.' (Strang 2004: 52) Water, in other words, seems to possess many sensuous qualities which have the potential to reach into spa visitors and lull their bodies and minds, conjoined with the outer surface of the skin as well as the inner organs of the eyes, ears, and nose. And as it does this, it informs the visitor's body, consciously and unconsciously, that s/he is in a unique place that is qualitatively different from most everyday settings.

In line with this, it might be argued that the primary commodities that places such as Varberg Kurort and Hasseludden have to offer are an alteric time and space in which patrons are temporarily isolated from all outside disturbances, and in which time, as well as the pace of daily life, is slowed down. This is a dominant image in the promotional material of spas; it is one of the central ambitions that spa managers claim they strive to provide, and as I have indicated above, it is at least in part one of the potential consequences that the spatial organization of spas may have upon visitors.

However, when viewed from a slightly different perspective, it might be argued that spas expend a great deal of effort setting things in motion rather than endeavoring to slow them down. Bodies are mobilized through organized activities such as spinning, power yoga, boxing, hiking, Nordic walking, weightlifting, and water aerobics. Working in more subtle ways, efforts are continuously made to mobilize new flows of energy via the massaging and stroking of bodies. In other words, in the world of spas the power of tactile stimulation is believed to free untapped, locked-up energies within, setting them in motion.[6] In this case, the caressing of the surface of the body cuts right to the core of the neurological system and works directly upon the stressed and stress-producing units of the body – this is, at least, what people in one way or another say they feel.

Interestingly, in spas the phenomenon of touch itself seems to be mobile, for the aura of the massage-rooms has a way of unfolding into the larger space of the spa. As couples enter spa reception areas and proceed into lounge areas, waiting-rooms, and bathing facilities, they are encompassed by a space of tactile intimacy that seems to pull them together. Here, couples are continuously placing their arms around one another's shoulders, and waists, rubbing and patting each other's backs, gently pecking one another on the lips or cheeks, running their fingers through each other's hair. Intimacy is tangibly present in this context, quite literally, but reading these signs of affection as muted forms of sexuality would be an oversimplification of the phenomenon at hand. Sexuality may be one of the forces pulling couples together in spas in some cases.[7] However, as noted in the previous chapter, sexuality is a force that works counter to the ideals of calm, relaxation, and harmony that spas strive to achieve. And indeed, spas go to great lengths to control this force – the material organization of the spas in question here leans towards an esthetic impression that could more accurately be described as being clinically or spiritually endowed than romantically laced. But as couples move through the spa, they recline in lounge chairs placed close to one another, bathe in jacuzzis that do not allow for great distance, and continuously hand each other cups of water or plates of fruit. The potential for physical contact is never far away.

However, my point is that this not a context in which people are continuously bumping into one another by accident. It is a context in which they actively reach out to each other. The power of touch in these cases works as an act of communication. It signals a relaxed stance towards those to whom it is directed, and seems to spread through the spa, almost contagiously – not only signaling relaxation, but facilitating it as well. It is, if nothing else, a confirmation of a relationship, and as such it is a social phenomenon.

The processes at work here are not limited to couples. Beyond couples, one of the other more prominent constellations of spa-goers is comprised of small groups of women out to spend a day or two together. While the intensity of tactile interaction is lower than amongst couples, similar processes are nonetheless at work binding these groups together. As they talk, laugh, and confide in one another, their voices are lowered and their bodies are physically pulled in closer to one another as a spatial compensation for the subdued level of their voices – resulting once again in a form of intimate space. Like couples, these are groups that go to spas to be together. Consequently, they even tend to move together, from lounge chairs to pools to saunas and so on. Pats on the back, a tug

Water is an important asset in the spas' attempts to affect the emotional states of their visitors. Beyond its medicinal history, and associated beliefs in water's ability to heal the body, the aural and visual quality of water is somewhat special. Aurally possessing a calming quality, its visual impact also has the capability of mesmerizing through its ability to reflect light, and function almost as a light source in and of itself. Photo: Tom O'Dell.

on an arm to get someone's attention, a touch on the shoulder; these are all small tactile gestures which go largely unnoticed but which nonetheless signal a relaxed sense of cohesion.

The touch, lowered voices, and focus on the specific person or group of people one has come to the spa with, all work to produce the sensation of an intimate atmosphere, but do so by focusing attention inwardly upon the group in question, and by implicitly erecting barriers between the group and others at the spa. Between groups, there is very little interaction. Each constellation of spa-goers is a bubble unto itself. To the extent that these groups have contact, it could be likened to a temporary popping of the bubble. A voice from another group that is too loud and affords a glance or stare, the entry of a second group into the jacuzzi which immediately makes the experience less intimate for the first group there, the overcrowding of a relaxation room, which with the entry of every new couple or group of patrons makes it feel more and more like the poolside environment at a charter resort than a private, intimate experience; these are all the types of intrusion that small groups of guests disdain and try to avoid by physically maximizing the distance between themselves and other groups in the spa. The ability to succeed in this endeavor is facilitated by the spa's division into a series of rooms, pools, saunas, and dining locations. The bubble of each group can remain intact, in short, as long as it continues to circulate, and half unconsciously feels the presence of others and reacts in response to that presence. What is at work here is affect at the cultural and social level. Decisions about what to do from moment to moment do not have to be discussed in detail or thoroughly analyzed, because intuitively the realm of possibilities for 'making the best of the situation' is ever felt.

On one level, the promise of health, wellness, and rejuvenation that spas make in their promotional material can seem to be highly ephemeral. In print, they are often reduced to representing this through the invocation of symbolically laden visual aesthetics that may signal wellness in one way or another, but say very little about how they actually achieve this goal. As a result, Varberg Kurort's promotional material is full of images of Swedish nature that harp on a discourse of 'being closer to nature' (and implicitly further from the stresses of modern urban life). Similarly, Hasseludden continuously reiterates its loyalty to its Japanese theme, and the message 'simpler is better' shines through, but the connection between Japanese design aesthetics and better health remains highly abstract. As I argue here, however, an understanding of the complex processes of cultural production that spas are engaged in begs for an analysis that moves beyond the text.

Spas have a materiality that not only shapes the experiences of people who move about within their confines, but this materiality 'matters' (Miller 1998b) because it has a way of mapping itself into the bodies of patrons. By stimulating the senses, it creates impressions and emotions, and informs consciousness – potentially affecting visitors in ways that may not always be completely apparent to them. Understanding the role of the body and senses in this context is important because, while our senses play an enormously important role in shaping conscious thought, a very large portion of the impulses and information that we process works below the radar of conscious thought. As Lakoff & Johnson have argued:

> Conscious thought is the tip of an enormous iceberg. It is the rule of thumb among cognitive scientists that unconscious thought is 95 percent of all thought – and that may be a serious underestimate. Moreover, the 95 percent below the surface of conscious awareness shapes and structures all conscious thought. If the cognitive unconscious were not doing this shaping, there could be no conscious thought. (1999: 13; see also Thrift 2000b: 40)

In this context, the spa is not only a place of health and leisure consumed by patrons, but through its material organization manipulates the senses, stimulating different forms and tempos of mobility and immobility in its attempt to affect the moods and emotions of patrons. To the extent that it succeeds in making visitors feel reinvigorated, it does so through a rich multiplicity of sensory cues that are registered only partially consciously in the minds of guests. It is the 'feel of the experience' that is more important here than any logical understanding or awareness of it. But at the same time, the space of the spa is not simply something that is designed and orchestrated from above by the spa's management; it is also created as people move through it and produce competing understandings of it. Let me expand upon this point by first turning to the corporeal activities of those working in spas, and the material organization of their work. Following this, I shall return to take one more look at the guests and the question of what they are actually doing as they relax. My ambition here is to focus on processes of kinesthesis and the effects the cultural framing of bodily movement can have in relation to perceptions of health.

Organizational space and mobile bodies

> There is no Good or Evil, but there is good and bad … The good is when a body directly compounds its relation with ours, and with all or part of its power, increases ours … For us, the bad is when a body decomposes our body's relation, although it still combines

with our parts, but in ways that do not correspond to our essence, as when a poison breaks down the blood. Hence good and bad have a primary, objective meaning, but one that is relative and partial: that which agrees with our nature or does not agree with it. (Deleuze 1988: 22)

Behind the scenes at spas one finds a very different taxonomy of corporeal rhythms of movement than those described above. The spas that are under consideration here are bound to hotel facilities. However, the organization of a spa is very different from the organization of an ordinary hotel.

In a hotel a limited number of employees are expected to be able to meet the demands and needs of a rather larger number of rooms and guests. Cleaning staff move in serial fashion from room to room, re-organizing, disinfecting, and tidying up the living spaces of dozens of people over the course of a day. Generally, they move from room to room, but when need be they can break this rhythm to deliver a glass, towel, or other service to a guest or colleague asking for help. Waiters and waitresses in the hotel restaurant share a similar capacity to move between tables quickly and flexibly, serving many people at once. The ability of the workforce in a hotel to function in this way is a prerequisite for the success of a hotel. The objective here from a management perspective is to fill up as many rooms and dining-room table spaces as possible, and to then find the right balance between the number of guests they have to serve, and the number of people employed to serve those guests satisfactorily. The exact ratio of guests to employees may vary slightly from hotel to hotel, but profitability hangs on the capacity of each employee to handle the needs and desires of several guests simultaneously.

Spas are different and surprisingly far more industrial in their organizational approach to hospitality than are hotels. A spa, for example, may feature eight massage and therapy rooms, two rooms for floating, a location or two for skin-care applications, and a reception area. In addition to this there may be pools, saunas, jacuzzis, and workout-rooms as well as relaxation areas. But in a spa, it is generally difficult to have one employee serving several areas and guests at once. On the contrary, when compared to a hotel, this is a personnel-intensive organization in which each person has a work station and is expected to produce at that station. Over the course of a day, a spa employee may move from one station to the next, as we shall see below, but nonetheless s/he has a specific place – at any given point in time – where s/he is expected to work on the body of the guest. One place, one employee, one space of production.[8] Further reifying this industrial order, masseuses, therapists or cosmeticians can only work on one person at a time. And it is only possible to work on one guest per room at a time (with the exception of couples who have booked a special 'couples' massage or treatment).

This reality places constraints upon spas and can cause problems for them. For example, it is not unusual for groups of three or four women book a spa visit for a 'girls' day out'. If two such groups book a spa visit on a Thursday, it can very well happen that all would like to have their treatments at the same time. Similarly, it is not unusual for couples visiting spas to request that their treatments be booked for the same time slot so that they can maximize the amount of time that they are together while still indulging themselves a bit. Yet Thursdays, like most days in the middle of a normal working week, are slow days for most spa hotels. Indeed, on a very slow day some of the spas where observations were conducted only served 8–12 people over the course of the day. The reason for this is that spa visitors generally stay for a full day of relaxation, or longer. Due to the rhythm of the working week, most people engage in this type of activity on the weekend rather than in the middle of the week.

And here we find a series of challenges for a spa facility. Labor costs are to some extent the Achilles heel of any spa facility. In order to meet this weekly rhythm it must employ a majority of its employees (who are primarily women) on a part-time basis, calling them to work when there is a demand for their services. A single skilled therapist might be able to take care of all 8–12 people over the course of a day, but this is only possible as long as each guest is treated one after the other, making it impossible to treat two guests simultaneously. If the spa calls in another therapist to work, it can now potentially offer visiting couples simultaneous treatments, but it merely has enough guests to keep two therapists occupied for half the day. And while a larger percentage of those who work at spas work on a part-time basis, those that do work often want to work for a full day in order to receive a full wage. Very few are interested in coming to work for an hour or less to treat a single guest. Indeed, many of the people employed in the industry have other part-time jobs which they must work into their schedules in order to earn enough money to survive on. One of the outcomes of this is that, while a hotel strives to fill all its rooms, a spa will strive to fill just a few rooms at a time. As more guests book treatments, more employees will be called into work, and more rooms opened for treatments. As each employee is called in to work, the spa strives to optimize the employment expectations of that individual in order to maximize their satisfaction with the facility as a place of work.

These constraints can create pressures, in different ways, for everyone working in the spa. From the perspective of a spa manager, the organizational strategy employed at a spa may help to keep down labor costs, but it can also create havoc when things do not go as planned. This became vividly apparent to me on one winter morning when I entered Scania Spa by the Sea, one of the spas in which I was conducting field-work, just prior to opening time. I found the spa manager huddled over a telephone, surrounded by three of her employees, studying the day's work schedule and frantically dialing numbers. What follows is an excerpt from my field-notes.

I smile and say, "Hi! How's it going?" Maria [the spa manager] looks a little uncomfortable. "Things are a bit chaotic … One of the therapists is sick. We're trying to reach some of our customers to offer them an alternative. It isn't easy."

"Don't you have anyone who lives around here whom you can call in?" I ask.

But she misunderstands me and says, "No, they live in Malmö, Lund –", looking at the names on the list of the day's activities and guests' names. She let's me know that she is worried that some customers might be disappointed, and this can cause tensions … She's hoping the day will turn out well, but is feeling the pressure now. "It's so damn hard", she says. She points to a name: "Have you called them?"

"Yes", answers one of the young women.

"Call again", says Maria.

"But I left a message", answers the young woman.
"Call again. It's better that we're thorough", says Maria.

The unexpected inability of a single therapist to come to work due
to sickness meant in essence that all of the treatments booked and
assigned to that person were jeopardized. As it turned out, Maria
failed to find a replacement for the sick therapist – and failed to
reach many of the visitors who had booked treatments and were
presumably on their way to the spa. Consequently, she spent the
better part of the day struggling to mitigate her guests' disappointment. One couple who had booked two hour-long massages were
informed that they could each receive a half-hour massage if they
wanted, or if one of them chose a different type of treatment such
as an hour of floating, then one of them could still receive the hour-
long massage. A number of other guests received similar news. Their
disappointment was tangible, but everyone seemed to overcome their
disappointment quickly. And all the while Maria kept smiling and
reassuringly pointing out new options as she gently coaxed visitors
to try other treatments than those they had scheduled. Only after
several hours of work, when the reception area was empty of guests,
did she turn to a member of the cleaning staff and say,

> You can never relax, because every day is a new situation … usu-
> ally, those who work part-time here have other jobs in other places
> … You can often work things out, but it's really tough, because
> you open at 9 a.m. and the first thing you have to do is ring to
> employees and customers.

But it is not only spa managers that feel the pressures of the job. On
another day at the same spa, I watched as Eva moved continuously
between the reception area where she met guests and greeted them
warmly, and the treatment rooms where she provided them with
their massages. She had explained to me that she had just recently
started working as a masseuse again after having left the industry
for a number of years. In her opinion this was a job that she could
only do for shorter periods of time before becoming too exhausted
to continue. A few months, and then she would probably have to

move on to a new job again, she explained. Reflecting upon her words, I was surprised when she suddenly appeared in the reception area in an aerobics outfit. She seemed hurried as she looked for a portable microphone behind the counter. Another masseuse in her early twenties smiled at her and said, "Don't you look sporty?" Whereupon Eva shot her an angry glance and hissed, "I mostly feel stressed out", before proceeding to the pool area to lead a water aerobics class. But over the course of my research, these proved to be a couple of the rare moments in which the phenomenon which Arlie Russell Hochschild calls 'emotion management' (2003: 87) broke down, revealing the tension that personnel could feel in a world that otherwise gave every semblance of calm.

The dynamics of this were made a bit clearer to me by Malin, a woman in her mid-twenties who had only worked at Scania Spa by the Sea for a few months when I spoke with her. Before beginning at Scania by the Sea, in order to qualify for her profession she had undergone a year-long private education which had included studies in anatomy, physiology, and cosmetology. When I asked her how her experience of working at a spa compared to her prior expectations, she explained that the work was 'heavier' than she had expected. She was glad that she had the job, but felt drained after working ten hours a day, four days a week. "Some people are so full of negative energy, which comes back at you," she explained, describing how she had to work almost like a psychologist, listening to people's stories, in an attempt to make them happy. "I get home and I am totally exhausted, but somehow you get charged up for the next day." And as she discussed the fact that most people did not, as far as she knew, work more than three years in the branch – "you just can't keep at it longer than that" – she did not hesitate before proceeding to describe how she looked forward to the future and dreamed of opening her own spa. She hoped this would provide her with a steady and regular clientele base which she could come to know well, and whose needs she would thus be better able to meet.

In short, spas and the people working in them are extremely adept at portraying themselves as the essence of calm and tranquillity, but as one branch publication explained, 'Spas give you the impression of being about luxury, but no one in the field is strong enough to work full-time. At the same time, they have to make a living, so they keep on working.' (Kellner, 2003: 22) The physical and emotional weight of the job proves, all too often, to be too much for staff to continue for longer periods of time. This is a problem that spa managers are aware of, and for which they have developed a number of different strategies with which they hope to handle the tension between their needs for personnel on a flexible basis, and the problems of working those employees too hard. Some spas have enlisted an on-call system in which employees are guaranteed certain weekends off, but are left on-call on other weekends. Since weekends tend to be the busiest time of the week for spas, it is not uncommon for employees who are on-call to find themselves working those weekends when they would otherwise have had time to recuperate from their work.

Other spa managers have opted to implement different strategies to solve their personnel problems. For example, Wilderness Spa and Retreat,[9] another of Sweden's larger spas, opted to rely heavily upon young women who came directly from a variety of masseuse training programs, and put them to work full-time. The result was that many quit their jobs within a year (*Svensk Hotellrevy*, 2003: 23). In this case, management seemed to have come to the conclusion that it was easier to replace worn-out employees than to make their working routines bearable.

A third spa strove to prevent their employees from burning out by encouraging those who engaged in strenuous activities to perform less physically demanding tasks such as receptionist duties or serving in the facility's restaurant. While the management's intentions were perhaps good, employees resisted the strategy. The problem here was that many of the employees in question had invested time and money in special educational programs to become masseuses and therapists. The suggestion that they answer telephones or wait on tables was perceived as degrading, and threatened perceptions of their own occupational identity.

Spas are labyrinths of mobile bodies. In the worst cases they are sites of stress production, with a revolving-door policy that consumes bodies, wearing them out and ultimately discarding them. In other cases, attempts are made to avoid this by employing people on a part-time and flexible basis, or through attempts to transfer them between different types of tasks. Whatever the case, the work being performed at spas has to be carefully organized. Work schedules divided into days, half-days, weekends, and evenings steer the constant flow of bodies between employment positions and homes. Even more detailed schedules divide the working day up into ever smaller units of time, clearly defining who will be working in specific treatment rooms, and who will be moving on to an aerobics class by the pool, or a yoga class in another part of the facility.

This is not a flow that is limited to the bodies of employees. The guest's visit has a distinct rhythm of its own. And while spas do their very best to present themselves as places of relaxation, disconnected from the problems and stresses of the outside world, they are nonetheless intimately interconnected with the pulse of the larger cultural economy in more ways than one. Spas such as Varberg and Hasseludden can accommodate thousands of visitors every week. No single service could meet the wishes of all these clients. Consequently, larger spas such as these have had to develop innovative and creative strategies for delivering mass services that seem to be entirely individualized. Varberg achieves this, in part, by 'mass customizing' its product (cf. O'Dell 2005b & 2005d; Pine & Gilmore, 1999 & 1998); the resort meets the desires of its clients by offering a standardized but wide range of treatments and activities that people can choose from, combine, and put together in a manner that allows them to produce their own individualized experience.

The package deals that Varberg offers constitute one way of handling this organizational need, allowing the spa management to calculate more easily room vacancies in advance, as well as to anticipate personnel requirements in meeting the shifting demand for meals, treatments, and other activities in the spa's immediate future. Another organizational technique comes in the form of a timetable called an 'activities menu'. The menu divides each day into blocks of time ranging from 30 to 60 minutes, with the activity or treatment patrons can participate in at any given time on any day. A sign-up sheet is posted in the spa's lobby that specifies the number of people who can participate in each activity. So, on Monday morning the schedule lists:

07.30–08.00   Oriental morning
08.30–09.00 H_2O-Spinning
09.15–09.45 H_2O
10.15–11.00   Qi Gymnastics
11.15–12.15   Yoga

No two days offer exactly the same schedule, and the rule of first-come first-served applies to many of the activities on the sign-up sheet. While relaxation is the goal, the clock rules here in much the same way as it has throughout the industrial era. The difference in this case lies in the fact that 'spa time' is more cyclical than linear in nature. If you miss a specific activity that you have been looking forward to, it is bound to reappear on the schedule in the coming days. In other words, it is still available to you if you stay long enough. In the end, however, it is through processes of internalized discipline – which were themselves honed and developed with the advent of the industrial era – that the spa and its patrons work to alleviate stress and burnout.

Time is of the essence. Meals are served within the span of rather exact time periods, and treatments are measured in minutes. Varberg instructs its guests to arrive at their pre-ordered treatments five minutes ahead of schedule. By spa standards, these are rather lax time constraints. Other spas go as far as to demand your presence fifteen minutes in advance of your massage or treatment, and can even explicitly warn that lateness will be deducted from the time of your treatment. In other words, it is the consumer and not only the laborer/producer who has the responsibility of watching the clock and meeting time requirements. The spa is presumed to function like a well-ordered institution in which its employees are in their places and waiting for the next scheduled production unit to pass through. The greatest threat to this order is the undisciplined body of the visitor that finds itself unable to keep to the agreed schedule. Discipline is essential to the functioning of this machine. Backlogs in production simply cannot occur, as they threaten the quality of the product provided to the next customer.

At Varberg, work schedules, activities menus, and package deals are crucial organizational instruments that help the spa facilitate a regime of flexibility that keeps both patrons and employees on the go – moving them from room to room, providing them with a series of activities to keep them busy, and clearly defining the stations and time-frames in which to perform their work (or leisure). Other cultural theorists have assertively argued for the need to appreciate the capacity of flexibility to 'arouse anxiety' (Sennett 1998: 9) and 'uncertainty' (Bauman 2000: 147) within the ranks of the labor market. These are aspects of working-place flexibility that spa employees face; somewhat paradoxically, however, it is also in their exposure to similar processes and organizational strategies that spa patrons strive to flee stress and anxiety, and in many cases claim to succeed in this. Regimes of flexibility, it seems, do more than produce stress.

Elsewhere (O'Dell 2004 & 2005c) I have argued for a need to better understand the kinesthetic tension between cultural processes of stasis and mobility, and the manner in which they become morally charged in daily life (see also Klinkmann 2005).[10] By juxtaposing the work schedules of spa employees with the activity schedules offered to visitors, my intention here is to argue for a need to further interrogate the question of what the demands (and expectations) of flexibility and mobility do with us in shifting contexts. Why do regimes of flexibility and mobility seem to 'break people down' in some contexts, but 'build them up' in others? As I have argued throughout this book, spas endeavor to induce serenity and recharge their patrons by carefully managing processes of cultural kinesthesis, targeting guests' bodies and senses to affect their emotions and feelings by continuously working competing modes of mobility and stasis in a morally charged context that is defined in terms of wellness, health, and (via the Protestant ethic) increased economic productivity. Interestingly, corporeal tempos of activity, which are generally associated with productivity in working life, are re-invoked and re-contextualized in many of Sweden's spas in a manner that (perhaps not so surprisingly) seems to reassure guests of the facility's ability to have a productive and rejuvenating effect upon them.[11] This may seem paradoxical, even 'illogical', but to the extent that it works, it does so because it all makes sense to the body, at some level. And this is perhaps what is most important in this context.

We live in a world in which our consciousness lags after us by

0.8–1.5 seconds (Nørretranders 1998: 215; Thrift 2004: 67). In targeting our senses, spas (and many other actors within the experience economy) are essentially engaged in a project that aims to colonize the pre-reflexive gap between our bodies and our consciousness, working to affect the latter through the former. Meaning, in this context, is communicated not solely by words, text, or language, but more importantly through the corporeal impressions generated from spatial practices (Lefebvre's first space, 1991: 38; see also Merrifield 2000: 174 ff.; Soja 1996: 66). As patrons intuitively dispose themselves towards relaxation and pampering, they open their senses and partake of the spa's surroundings. As they do so, their senses, like a slew of probing tentacles and antennae, are constantly extending out into the surrounding world of well-being, gathering information about it. And even before they are fully aware of the implications of this information, their bodies relate to it.

But as Malin's words above illustrate, the bodies and souls of spa patrons do not only reach out into the material world of the spa, absorbing emotional stimulus from it. They also have the potential to reach out and affect the world around them, giving it form even as they are affected by it. As part of this process, spa guests transfer part of the emotional residue they have brought with them to the spa to the bodies of those who are employed to care of them. Coming to work each day, having found a way to 'recharge' overnight, people like Malin strive to inject their visitors with new energy and a sense of wellness. In return, part of what they receive is the stress, tension, unease, and everything Malin describes as the 'bad energy' of the bodies lying prone before them – an energy which guests have brought with them from society at large. Thus, as spas hone their techniques of colonizing the pre-reflexive gap of their guests, they find themselves struggling with the problem of their guests' ability to colonize the souls of their employees through that very same gap.

The situation is further complicated by the manner in which the material and spatial organization of the spa has a way of working in conjunction with the bodily practices of its personnel to wear away at the enthusiasm which brings so many young women to want to work at spas. As work schedules are filled, a steady flow of bodies are cared for, rubbed, and massaged. The oil that brings comfort to the guest is the same oil (with the same scent) that the masseuse uses over and over again – that ultimately contributes to the production of sore fingers, hands, and arms in spa personnel. The rites of relaxation discussed here and in the previous chapter have an effect because they are ritualistically performed over and over again in a manner that exudes a sense of professional calm. However, their repetitiveness has consequences as ten-hour days turn into months of work, and as poolside aerobics classes melt into full-body massages, spinning sessions, and facials. The spa does not only work its way into the bodies of guests, but even into the bodies of its own personnel, through a series of daily routines that leaves employees moving about (and all too often burning out) at an ever more frantic tempo that is thinly but effectively concealed by processes of emotional management.

These are the conditions under which spa directors, managers, and employees have to work. The secret to working magic is the secret of mastering a period of time that is a little less than a second in duration. In order to truly succeed, guests should only vaguely, if at all, be aware of what is happening in that split second. It implies that guests should not be fully aware of how the spa is working on them, but also that they have to remain completely oblivious to the ways in which they (and the spa at large) are affecting the employees around them. An awareness, on the part of the guests, of any level of stress amongst employees would dissolve the magical effects of the spa immediately. Few Swedes attending a spa would be unmoved by the realization that the woman taking care of them at that moment was also working to cope with the stress of the job quite literally in hand.

The total elimination of this stress would be an optimal point of departure for any spa manager (the existence of stress, or the slightest sign of it in anyone in the spa, is in many ways the great-est threat to the spa), but as indicated above, this is not a problem with quick and easy solutions that neatly coincide with ambitions of economic efficiency. Until such an optimal solution is found (if it can be found), the ability of spas to endow their guests with a sense of serenity will be intimately connected with their ability to dissipate any and all signs of stress. Controlling the powers and processes of invisibility are in other words important prerequisites to the making of a hospitable space for the soul within the auspices of today's wellness industry. But it also places specific conditions on all who enter this space. And here it is possible to discern slight differences in the cultural organization of hospitality today when compared to the contours of its nineteenth-century predecessor.

Hospitality and invisibility

Take the case of Ramlösa Hälsobrunn which was discussed in chapter two, for example. Ramlösa Hälsobrunn was a place in which very different groups of guests were always present, but organized in a manner that diminished the degree of their interaction. And while they may not have socialized much together, they did at least share a limited degree of mutual recognition of one another. The impoverished were recognized as having a right to access the waters of the spa, and efforts were made to raise funds that made it possible for them to spend time at the facility. Today, the market mechanism of pricing works to diminish the diversity of the guest population at most Swedish spas,[12] as does the promotional imagery that they use to attract customers. However, the line of difference that exists between staff and guests is still a point of potential tension that spas must contend with. The use of uniforms, professional language, 'staff only' areas of access, and ritualized means of beginning and ending treatments are all used to help create and maintain the 'right atmosphere' – for the reception of this particular form of commercialized hospitality – but they do so by disguising class differences, economic inequalities, hierarchies of servitude, the stress of work schedules, and the potential physical frailties of staff members. All the while, the time schedules discussed in this chapter keep everyone moving, but in slightly different circles, and through slightly different spaces of the spa – minimizing the chance that guests should ever be reminded of the degree to which their well-being might be related to the different life circumstances of those serving them. In this sense, the regimes of mobility set in motion at spas assure the fact that staff members are both tolerated and accepted by guests, but not necessarily *recognized* by them. And this is important, because as Mustafa Dikeç has argued:

> Thinking about hospitality is not only to think about a generous and cordial welcome. Thinking about hospitality, more importantly, is to think about *openings* and *recognition*. Although boundaries form an inherent part of the notion of hospitality, without which such a notion would perhaps be unnecessary, hospitality, I want to argue, is about opening without abolishing these boundaries and *giving spaces* to the stranger where recognition on both sides would be possible. (Dikeç 2002: 229)

Where nineteenth-century spa guests at Ramlösa raised money for the poor, produced newspapers, and engaged in other activities to contribute to the pension funds of spa personnel, spas today work effectively as 'smoothing machines' (Deleuze & Guattari 1987: 474 ff.), disguising and removing signs of difference. They have to, because the magic of relaxation would be shattered if guests were confronted by complaining employees. The invisibility of the Other's life circumstances is, it would seem, something of a precondition for the maintenance of a façade of conditional hospitality at Swedish spas.

This is nothing new. Invisibility has long been presumed to be an 'ideal' quality in servants. But if spas are a part of anything that might be referred to as a hospitality industry, it is apparent that the conditions of the 'conditional hospitality' that they offer have hardened. Where guests could hardly avoid recognizing the presence of others, and acknowledged (at least in limited ways) the right of those others to exist at the spa in the nineteenth century, they are increasingly preoccupied with the question of their own affect and well-being today. But a focus upon questions of well-being and affect implies an acute attention to the details of the present (cf. Thrift 2000b) – to the question of how do I feel now in the jacuzzi, how do I feel now in the sauna, how do I feel now on the massage table? But as I am arguing here, wellness is not just a frame of mind. In order to become a feeling in the body, it has to be enacted and lived (Damasio 2003). It is through the body's movement from place to place, from the one experience to the other, that it is able to approach a feeling of wellness – through engagement with the rituals of well-being – although the processes involved here are reinforced as couples and individuals in small groups reflect upon their feelings and discuss them with one another.[13]

Against this background, it is perhaps unsurprising to find that the life circumstances of others are missing from the radar screens of today's spa guests. They are engaged in a cultural sphere of activity that is defined, on the one hand, in terms of their hosts' ability to focus upon them, and on the other hand by their own ability to introspectively monitor and control their own feelings – to calm down, 'find harmony', and enjoy the feeling of being pampered. Lifting one's gaze to observe the life circumstances of those in one's proximity would be an act which broke with the cultural grammar of the spa. Thus, to the extent that hospitality can be understood as being comprised by a relationship between guests and hosts, this relationship has become extraordinarily one-sided. This is a world in which guests are increasingly searching the market (and relying upon it, engaging in a different and particular relationship with it instead of with particular individuals) for hospitable openings into the realm of well-being. It is perhaps not illogical that they expect that same market to be able to meet the needs of those caring for them – all the cultural cues around them, after all, exude an atmosphere of well-being, and on the surface of things this seems to include spa employees. The problem is that the market-driven realities in which spas operate are no different from the realities that have driven guests to seek refuge (and the hands of others) in the spa.

As guests leave the spa, however, they are faced with a new question, 'How can I maintain this feeling?' In the following chapter I turn to the home to reflect upon the effects the market for wellness might be having upon daily life. As it transpires, the ideals and dreams of well-being embedded in the spa – and mechanisms driving its expansion – are not limited to it. Over the course of the first years of the new millennium they came increasingly to seep into society at large, as consumers searched for new spaces of hospitality and spiritual regeneration on market shelves, and in bathroom supply stores. But to better understand this, let's go home.

CHAPTER 5

Bringing the Spa Home

Any period of great cultural change will also be a time of sensory confusion, for social revolutions are always sensory revolutions.

(Howes 2005b: 11).

My favorite time of the day is when I sink down into a bath. My bath-tub isn't particularly big, but it takes up about a third of my bathroom. It's classic white and sits a little bit above the floor like a water-filled hammock. Besides water, a bathroom has to have good lighting (a dimmer is essential!), some space for candles and incense, and if possible, a sound-proof door. (Nestius 2006: 4)

Private habits are constructed as people steer their own course through culturally and temporally specific landscapes of legitimating discourse and classifications of ordinary and extraordinary behaviour.

(Shove 2003: 94)

On March 2, 2007, I found myself browsing the shelves of a Florida toy-store looking for a birthday present for my four-year-old daughter. Wedged between the Disgusting Science science kit and another kit featuring over 1,500 experiments, I found something that was perhaps not the perfect gift for the occasion in mind, but it at least caught my eye: the Scientific Explorer Spa Science kit. The lid promised that this was 'real chemistry', a kit which would allow young explorers to 'relax and experiment with different fragrances in your bath', by creating 'your own secret formulas'. Anyone concerned at the thought of their children conducting 'real chemistry' in an attempt to create new fragrances at home could find solace on the back of the box. As it explained, the kit included 'recipes from nature' that would help the young chemist (ages 9 and up) 'blend natural and organic ingredients to make your own fresh spa products'. In addi-

The Scientific Explorer Spa Science kit: a gendered training ground that brings the experience economy home and introduces young girls to the sensual world of spas. Photo: Tom O'Dell.

tion to plastic pipettes, a test tube, some cups, instructions, and a book of experiments, the kit included a few small bags each with its own contents: rosebuds, oats, sea-salt, baking soda, and lavender, as well as peppermint oil. Herein lies the essence of the home spa experience, at least from Scientific Explorer's perspective. Peeking into the box, the small white envelopes containing a few ounces of oats, salts, and baking soda seemed anything but magical, but the twenty-dollar price tag almost assured me that those small white envelopes had to be hiding something more than just ordinary oats and salts. Each envelope bore a silent promise of opening a new world of unique sensory experience for some lucky future chemist.

Like most toys, this was a training kit for adulthood, offering young girls a set of props with which they could begin to experiment with new identities and possibilities for the future. But like most toys, it was also a cultural marker attesting to the values, attitudes, and expectations which parents and other adults deemed particularly worthy of transferring on to a younger generation of children. One parent who purchased the kit from Amazon.com described the kit as follows:

> Spa Science is probably more of a recipe than a science experiment, but is still a lot of fun. Girls mix fragrances and bases into fun bath

prodcuts. Some fizz and release bubbles (carbon dioxide-hense the science part). My 10 yr old dughter enjoys mixing things and creating new blends of ingredients, so this kit was right up her alley. Alot of fun for all girls. It may transfer into an interest in science, but science is not the main focus of the kit.[1]

Even if the level of education and scientific knowledge that the kit had to offer could be questioned, the kit was if nothing else a gendered training ground in which young girls could take a couple of steps further into the commercialized market of affect, under adult supervision, and without ever leaving the bounds of the home. The kit may very well be 'a lot of fun for all girls', as the parent above phrased it, but it is also interesting for the degree to which it helps illustrate one of the many small ways in which the processes which economists such as Pine and Gilmore (1999) discuss in a market context, bound to the public sphere, are also intimately entwined in people's private lives and domestic settings. The experience economy is more than a public matter.

In what follows, my intention is to follow the processes at work here into the home to analyze the manner in which they are leaving their mark there. In order to do this, I shall repeatedly move between the public sphere of the spa and the private sphere of the home, but the focus will be upon processes at work in the home. After all, the phenomena that I have described in the preceding chapters are not limited to spas. Spas just happen to be good places in which to study them, and to develop a better understanding of many of the more important processes at work in the cultural economy. But these processes are at work throughout society, often in ways to which we are almost completely oblivious. Indeed, in stating that my ambition is to follow these processes into the home I may in some ways be misrepresenting what is actually happening, alluding to a movement from the outside inwards (from the spa to the home). Within the context of this book, the empirical material that this chapter builds upon does move from the spa to the home, for in reality the home works well as a laboratory of experimentation, in which inconspicuous daily practices can have effects far beyond the home. The case may be that spas begin to take shape here, in the home, and develop from the lessons we have already learned here, through both the daily practices and symbolic interpretations we engage in behind closed doors.

Sensescaping the home

In 2001 the Swedish interior design magazine *Sköna hem*, offered readers a glimpse of the luxurious life available at three spas located in different parts of the world: one in Sweden, one in Switzerland, and one in the Maldives. Holding true to their interior design focus, they concluded the article with several pages of tips on how similar sensations of luxury to those described in the preceding pages could be achieved in the confines of one's very own home – for considerably less money. As they explained:

> Enjoy yourself in your own spa. All bathrooms have spa potential, and with a little preparation and comforting products it's possible to enjoy a spa in your own home environment – even if it's on a slightly different scale. Here are the tips that will increase your pleasure in the bathroom. (Hed 2001: 129)

What followed was a smorgasbord of the rather modest elements needed to convert an ordinary bathroom into the private equivalent of a modern luxury spa. Fresh flowers and a warm footbath 'to spoil yourself' with, shower heads with massage functions, 'refreshing' oils, 'softening' soaps, and designer soap bowls that could 'lift' the entire aesthetic experience (ibid.: 129 ff.). The article was in part a thinly disguised advertisement for a diverse array of bathroom products, but it was also the equivalent of a magician's handbook, taking readers step-by-step through the art of reorganizing both their homes and their reflexive orientations toward themselves – all in the name of optimizing their potential to obtain an altered state of affect.

A few years later *Better Homes and Gardens* published a special edition of its magazine which, under the heading 'MindBodySpirit', pushed this focus upon the self and the senses even further. The magazine's cover featured a call to readers to 'Pamper yourself with at-home spa ideas', placed beside an image of soft terry cloth towels and soaps tied in silk ribbons. In opening, the magazine explained,

When you indulge in a luxurious bath, you give yourself a gift and become part of the time-honored tradition of using water – simple water – as a restorative tool to wash away daily cares.

Both department stores and small boutiques offer huge selections of scented candles, pot-pourri mixes, and plush towels to make the ritual bath a more sensual experience. Mass merchandisers have even packaged the sounds of gently bubbling brooks and sell soothing relaxation fountains with gentle water sounds to add to the relaxing environment. (*Better Homes and Gardens* 2003: 13)

In the following pages, the magazine provided careful instructions on how to go about creating ritual baths that provide 'respite for the soul' and 'strengthen the spirit' (ibid.). Candles should be lit to provide the warmth of a low light and thereby a feeling of calm. Special towels, brushes, and soaps were to be used to provide the optimal 'high-touch experience' (ibid.: 14). The sounds of brooks and fountains could be purchased to reinforce the calming powers of the bath ritual. And throughout the description, a whirlwind of olfactory stimulation positively leapt from the page in the form of scented soaps, candles, oils, petals, fruits, and pot-pourri. The key to success seemed to lie in not only an acute attention to the smallest of sensuous details, but more importantly in a strong awareness of them. And while the examples taken here come from Swedish and American magazines, they are increasingly to be found in similar types of magazines published around the world.

At issue here are the processes involved in a phenomenon which Nigel Thrift has referred to as 'a new structure of attention' (2004: 67): a way of seeing the world, of focusing on the smallest of details and activities that are taking place in the half-second delay between present time and the formation of consciousness. As Thrift argues, this new structure of attention bears with it a growing awareness and appreciation of the possibility of influencing the way in which people anticipate the world, and intuitively orient themselves towards it, by concentrating and delivering new forms of non-verbal communication to the pre-reflexive gap.

To some extent it might be argued that this is not a new structure at all. Marketers working decades ago strove to influence consumers by clipping a single frame of film showing a soft drink or popcorn into movie reels. The thought was that by doing so, they could influence people to purchase those products. The degree to which this particular technique actually worked was hotly debated and remains contested to this day. However, this has not curbed the interest of marketers, manufacturers, and others in prying deeper into the realm of the body and senses to find new and effective ways to communicate and persuade. On the contrary, the pre-reflexive gap has come into view in new ways as realtors have learned that the smell of freshly baked bread makes it easier to sell a home, and automobile manufacturers have become aware of the importance that the feel of certain types of leather have for producing a convincing sense of luxury in consumers.

However, what is at issue here is not just marketing and economics. As Thrift points out with concern, this is also an issue of politics.

> What is being ushered in now is a *micro-biopolitics*, a new domain carved out of the half-second delay which has become visible and so available to be worked upon through a whole series of new entities and institutions. This domain was already implicitly political, most especially through the mechanics of the various body positions which are a part of its multiple abilities to anticipate. Now it has become explicitly political through practices and techniques which are aimed at it specifically. (Thrift 2004: 67)

Thrift sees the processes at work here as a kind of 'landscape engineering' (ibid.: 68) that is focused upon the geography of the body and senses, as actors ranging from politicians and city planners to marketers and manufacturers attempt to convince us (of whatever they are arguing for) through subtle appeals to our senses and emotions. And while he does offer a series of emancipatory directions in which a politics of affect could be developed, he fails to address fully what might be the most important factor at work here: the fact that people are not only being targeted by affective messages, but that they are also in search of them. Indeed, they are constantly developing new competencies with which to focus their attention on the processes at work in the half-second delay in consciousness, at the same time as this increasing focus also provides them with the opportunity to control and steer parts of those processes.

More than hygiene

In this context it is interesting to note the shifting significance accorded the bathroom in a European country such as Sweden. As ethnologist Klas Ramberg has pointed out, apartments without bathrooms were still being constructed in Sweden as late as the mid-1930s (Ramberg 2004: 120). If you speak to Swedes who lived in centrally located apartments in many of the country's larger cities, it is not uncommon to hear stories of people who lived without bathrooms in their apartments well into the 1970s. Shower and bathing facilities were located in the basements of these buildings, and shared by all living there. The move to install a bathroom into the apartment may have represented a form of luxury in this context, but more than anything, it was a drastic improvement in convenience.

Home-owners had an advantage, being able to adjust their homes more quickly and flexibly to the latest trends. Even so, I have memories of as a child visiting my grandmother in the 1960s and 1970s, making the trip down the cold stone stairs to the basement of her home to a tub located in the corner of a basement room. The coldness of the cement walls and floors was broken only by the wooden crate tops she had laid out next to the bathtub as an improvised form of flooring that at least kept me off of the concrete floor as I dried myself off after my bath. My grandmother was perhaps not the most trend-sensitive woman in southern Sweden, but her bathroom would not have been viewed as particularly odd in the early 1970s, even if much better alternatives already existed on reasonably widespread basis.

More fashionable Swedes in the late 1960s and early 1970s (well, those with more modern bathroom facilities than my grandmother's) fulfilled their bathing fantasies by investing in home saunas and swimming pools. The saunas of this era were not presented as an opportunity for self-pampering, however. On the contrary, they straddled a border between the slightly erotic and the mundanely domestic. Advertisements often featured bare-breasted women lounging in poses of absolute relaxation and self-abandon. This may have been a world of sexual possibilities, but it was a controlled and domesticated form of sexuality, a space in which one could assert one's self as a sexually 'cool', modern, and liberated Swede. It was a space for partners and families. 'Now my wife also takes saunas …

and our entire family thinks it's doubly wonderful taking saunas at home' was the hook Tylö saunas used to market its products (Tylö advertisement 1968), while Bacho saunas pictured a family horsing around and laughing in a sauna and explained: 'The Cozy Club is made up of dad, mom, and the kids. It meets at least one evening a week in 80°C temperatures and very informal clothing' (Bahco advertisement 1968: 12). Rather than focusing attention inwardly upon the individual experience one could have, Swedish sauna manufacturers presented their products as vehicles that could bring families together. As Jonas Frykman has pointed out in a reflection over the cultural history of the sauna in Sweden, 'The sauna was something you thought *with* when you imagined the good life' (2004: 102). And the good life here was slightly erotic, but firmly domestic.

Swimming pools of the era were presented in similar domestically pre-occupied terms. They were places in which families could interact, and parents could calmly watch as their children frolicked within arm's reach. The largest problem that pool manufacturers faced was that of being stamped as a form of expensive luxury, and they went to great lengths to assert that their products were an affordable alternative for middle-class families. Ultimately, pools were never fully incorporated into the middle-class home to the extent of the sauna, and even the sauna's glory days were relatively short-lived. By the 1980s most Swedish saunas were either being used as oversized drying cabinets for the family's laundry, or had become the equivalent of an indoor storage shed for rarely used household goods.

Throughout it all, the bathroom failed to attract much attention. Indeed, if one surveys the interior design magazines from the 1960s to the 1980s, bathrooms are notable by their absence. While these magazines devoted large amounts of space to kitchens, living-rooms, and bedrooms, the bathroom was often entirely neglected or only given a very marginal position. Large articles dominated by photographs of stylistically 'correct' middle- and upper-middle-class homes absorbed page after page of a magazine's content without ever coming near the bathroom. When it was referred to, it tended to be in the advice columns of the magazines, as was the case of one home-owner who in 1988 lived in a ten-year-old home with a bathroom of less than four square meters. The problem which this person faced was not only that the bathroom was small, but that s/he could hardly get into the shower stall because the sink blocked the way. The question was how this problem could be solved by expanding the bathroom another sixty centimeters, at the cost of a closet.

The bathroom until this point generally filled a hygienic role, which was addressed in a highly functional manner. But in the letters home-owners sent to interior decorating magazines asking for advice on how to re-model their bathrooms, it is possible to discern a slow shift in the manner in which Swedes were viewing their bathrooms. Function and hygiene were not enough. The question was how one could get more out of a bathroom. Advertisements of the time highlighted extra-small toilets, or corner tubs that could provide new spatial solutions to the bathroom (Gustavsberg advertisement 1988: 39ff). Colorful tiling was increasingly advocated as a way of perking up an otherwise mundane white-tiled bathroom. And slowly but surely jacuzzis began to enter the scene. 'Beautiful to look at, of course. Fun to own. But also a physiological pleasure. And under the perfect surface there's technology High Tech In the art of bathing', was how one firm tried to market the sensual experience of the jacuzzi in 1989.[2] Where saunas had once been marketed as family products, the jacuzzi was more intimate. This was a world in which one could find couples bathing and cuddling together, or women reclining by themselves in bubbling water. And while references to 'physiological pleasures' were rather vague, everyone implicitly understood that frolicking children did not belong in the dream world of jacuzzis. Jacuzzis were mood machines for adults, not playgrounds for small children, even if many jacuzzis ultimately wound up as the latter. For most people living in Sweden in the late 1980s, however, jacuzzis remained nothing more than a fantasy. But this and the significance attached to the bathroom changed rapidly in the years around the new millennium.

Bigger, bubblier, and better

If we look back in history, bathing had something holy about it. But times change, and Lutheran efficiency took over. Enjoyment was displaced to the murky corners of daily life, placed somewhere between the front hall and garage.

Luckily, those times have gone by. The bathroom has once again regained its place as the center of the home. (Sanova bathroom advertisement 2005)

Enjoy a relaxing, warm bath. Let the water from the shower massage and stimulate your skin. Relax in a pleasant reclining chair and regain your strength. Without a doubt, the bathroom has become the home's pleasure zone, and more and more people are striving to make it both functional and comfortable. (Pettersson 1999: 59)

On January 24, 2008 *Vi i Villa* (Sweden's leading magazine for home-owners) published a report on the latest trends amongst Swedish home-owners. According to information they had gathered, more than 25 percent of all home-owners in Sweden were planning on refurbishing and renovating their bathrooms over the course of the coming year, of which 80 percent said they were thinking of enlarging their bathrooms, and nearly 25 per cent were hoping to install a jacuzzi.[3]

Where the bathroom had once been treated sparingly in home and interior design magazines, it had now come to take a highly visible and prominent position. Functional design was still an appreciated quality, but as the bathroom took center stage in the home, it was simultaneously clothed in a much richer and sensually oriented vocabulary. Bathrooms became bold, exotic, elegant, romantic, soothing, luxurious, and dream-like – to invoke just a few of the adjectives used to describe them. And there seemed to be just about as many ideas about what a bathroom could be as there were adjectives to describe it. A rumpus room for the kids, a place to entertain neighbors and friends, a place to kick back and enjoy a newly installed flat-screen television – these were all alternative uses for the bathroom for which one could find apostles in the wealth of articles being produced to help Swedes in their renovation efforts.[4] But these were not necessarily the most popular directions in which Swedes intended to move (only 3 per cent of the home-owners reporting their renovation plans to *Vi i Villa* were interested in installing a flat-screen television in their bathroom).

Increasingly, bathrooms were framed as places of recuperation and healing, and the reintroduction of nature to the bathroom was of utmost importance in symbolically realigning the bathroom in these terms. For the better part of a century bathrooms had been designed and built as a reaction to nature. They were intended to protect people from their own natural waste, as well as the effects of such natural phenomena as bacteria, dirt, lice, and a whole host of contagions and micro-organisms. The bathroom (followed shortly thereafter by the kitchen) was the closest thing to a laboratory that one could find in the home – the ultimate site of engagement in the science of hygiene. Innovation after innovation had been incorporated into the bathroom to force nature into retreat.[5] The ease with which smooth plastic surfaces could be cleaned led to their mass introduction to the bathroom in the 1960s and 1970s. This was the era of vinyl floors and counter-tops, while the removable plastic toilet seat represented such a remarkable hygienic advance in the 1960s that its inventor was awarded a prize for best plastic invention at the time (Broomé 2006). The fact that these items were inorganic was understood to be a highly positive quality in the battle of science over nature. But in the years around the new millennium, nature was in vogue, and back in the bathroom.

Back to nature

However, nature in this millennial context was no longer a potential threat. It was a comforting nature, a warm nature, a soothing nature. Stone, in particular, was a sought-after commodity. When *Vi i Villa* asked Swedish home-owners what they would most like to have in their bathrooms, the most common answer (given by 53 per cent of those answering) was that they wanted a tiled floor (*Vi i Villa* 2008). Where Swedes had once trodden wall-to-wall vinyl flooring, they were now walking across Mediterranean tiling warmed from beneath by heating coils. Large oak bath-tubs were the height of luxury, and for those who could not afford them, other alternatives existed in the form of wooden cabinets and fittings, and wicker hampers. The ideal soap was handmade and included lavender, olive oil, or aloe vera. Rose petals, cinnamon sticks, or freshly cut flowers were all held up as ideal props to use in the furnishing of any bathroom with an appropriate aural texture. But this was by no

Where nature was once viewed as an unreliable force, capable of devastating people's lives by drought and famine, it is now often packaged as a mystically nurturing, healing, and soothing force. Here Palmolive endeavors to attract consumer interest through the invocation of nature's magical potential through references to seaweed extract and ylang-ylang oils. Family Fresh follow on with their 'ocean' and 'pearl dream'. Photo: Tom O'Dell.

means a movement limited to the world of those Swedes inclined to read interior-design magazines.

Even many of the larger global producers of bathroom products participated in the movement back to nature. In 2008, the shelves of an ordinary Swedish supermarket were lined with one nature-enhanced product after another. Palmolive, for example, offered a thermal spa soap with seaweed extract, an aromatherapy soap with 'pure essential oils of lavender, ylang-ylang and patchouli', another one with grapefruit, orange and cedar-wood, and a fourth with bergamot, cassis, and orange flower – all of which the Palmolive packaging promised would either 'relax', 'revitalize', or 'delight your senses'. Further down the shelf, the average shopper could find Family Fresh Ocean and Pearl Dream soaps, an assortment of Herbal Essences Rainforest Flowers shampoos, Garnier Fructis shampoos with 'reinforced active fruit concentrate', Gillette shaving cream with 'soothing aloe', and Naturelle anti-perspirant with either honey or peach depending on your mood. Even Bic disposable razors came with shaving heads with aloe and vitamin E. And in the section of the market devoted to toddlers, Natusan was presenting a new line of moisturizing lotions they called 'soothing naturals' that contained the oil of olive leaves, while Pampers offered wipes that were 'as mild as cotton wool and water', and laced with chamomile and aloe.

If nature had once been a dangerous threat that needed to be driven from the bathroom, it seems to have been rediscovered as a significant source of potential health. Spas regularly invoked images of nature to reinforce their own message of well-being. Nature could in this context symbolically work in diverse ways. As indicated in the previous chapter, nature partly represented a degree of separation from the bustle of daily life. But the placement of a stone in a spa, or the iconographic presentation of a sand-dune in a spa brochure also signified a degree of permanence, and slowness of time – nature being something which, in its pristine state, aged and changed very slowly (cf. Thrift 2000). All of this continues to be part of the aura of nature which spas draw into the fabric of their production – the magical power to resist time. And as people light lavender-scented candles, pour a warm bath, and lather up with soap containing cedar-wood oils, they are, at some level, partaking of this aura by adopting the 'new structure of attention' in an attempt conjure up a temporary spell of time resistance.

But more than this, they are calling upon the powers of nature to have a healing effect upon them. And thus, at some level, they are enlisting an underlying cultural understanding of the healing capacity of nature. True, there are long historical roots upon which beliefs in the curative effects of nature are based, but in addition to these historically anchored explanations, sociologist Jackie Stacy has pointed to a series of more modern factors underpinning contemporary perceptions of nature as a curative force. In part, she argues, they have been facilitated by a growing skepticism toward Western medicine which has gone hand in hand with an increasing willingness to experiment with alternative medicines (often of Eastern origin, and linked to Eastern philosophies of the mind and body) and natural medicines (including everything from ginseng to

St. John's wort). In part, they have been facilitated by the growing market for self-help and self-health literature. As Stacey explains:

> In many self-health books, readers are offered hope for a healthier future through a borrowing of beliefs and practices about disease and healing from non-western cultures. These cultures appeal because of their more natural approaches and their appropriate reverence for nature. Having lost faith in nature in the West, these non-western cultures are mobilised to re-authenticate the subject and to invigorate the body, or, indeed, to return it to its original, more natural, state. (2000: 119)

And in part, as hinted at here, they have been facilitated by the spread of Eastern and New Age philosophies which assert the interconnectedness of all living things, and the flow of energy between them. The mechanisms at work here may work in unison or they may work individually, but regardless, the combined effects of these processes have contributed to the development of a view of nature as a good, positive, and potentially healing force.

When Palmolive adds ylang-ylang to its soap, it is intentionally playing on these cultural strings and striving to invoke nature's magic. In saying this, my intention is not to deny or question the ability of some natural medicines to cure or diminish effects of a wide range of ailments. What I am trying to point out, however, is that the aloe on a Bic disposable razor is probably not going to cure that many diseases, but it is creating an aura of well-being by appealing to underlying cultural understandings of the power of nature – and the emotions those associations awaken in us. This aura is then brought home with every product appealing to the power of nature. The bathroom is not the only room in the house affected by these processes, but it is the space in the house most involved in them.

The image of the spa as a place of recuperation is an important part of this involvement, since the spa became the primary model which the ideal bathroom was supposed to emulate in the post-millennial years. However, the processes at work here did not necessarily require a visit to a spa to understand. The images of nature and emphasis upon sensory awareness that found expression in bathrooms at this time were related to what was happening in spas, but they were also part of a larger transnational flow of ideas and values in society at large (cf. Greenwood 2005; Stacey 2000 & Thrift 2000). The bathroom maintained its hygienic function, but it was also taking its first tentative steps toward a new role as a site of small-scale magical production and inner healing. From the hygienic functionality of the 1930s through the 1950s, it was becoming a room for relaxation and self-pampering – a place in which one could seek solitude as a means of fortifying oneself, as a means of ending a day or preparing for a new one (cf. Fredriksson 2006).

But the magic of this sensuous space was also the magic of opening a new hospitable space in the home. And the nature of this hospitable space is hidden in the smaller, less pronounced articles that were successively appearing in the same home and interior design magazines that highlighted the bathroom. Less conspicuous and more economically modest, there existed a parallel space in the home which women were working to open. A space called 'A Space For Myself'.[6] The struggle to open this space included a battle against a desk in a front hall, the temporary use of a kitchen table, or the need to retreat to the basement. It came to expression in magazines, home-improvement television programs, and the discourse of daily life. Implicitly, the counter-text of this discourse existed in the space of the husband or partner, and was often defined in terms of his den, his workshop, or his garage. It reflected the uneven rights of men and women to make claims of ownership over the spaces of the home. In this sense, the magic of the bathroom was also the magic of creating a hospitable space for oneself, particularly as a woman, and thus, like the spa itself, it had a gender bias.

In the early years of the new millennium Swedish spas attracted far more female than male patrons. This gender bias decreased steadily thereafter, but it never disappeared altogether.[7] When men did come to a spa, they often did so with their wives or partners, at their behest. Women I spoke with saw a spa visit as a means of relaxing and having fun with a friend or a spouse, but they also often described the visit as a form of welcome pampering or as an opportunity to be taken care of as they had cared for others.

The development of the home spa seemed to follow a similar pattern. It could easily be an expensive investment, so it was undoubtedly a renovation that families engaged in together, but information on how to furnish and organize a home spa, or how to create a spa experience on the cheap, was primarily directed towards women – often appearing in women's magazines as well as interior design magazines. As magazines such as *Sköna hem* and *Better Homes and Gardens* indicate, the production of a hospitable 'space for myself' did not have to be an extraordinarily intricate or expensive process (although it certainly could be both if one so desired). It just required a close attention to detail and an ability to navigate through the offerings of the market of 'well-being'. And in this sense, the details of the 'space for myself' were on the one hand the details of appropriating space by choice of materials and sensory organization, but on the other hand, and perhaps more importantly, they were the details of attending to oneself, of separating oneself from the demands of others (spouses, children, employers, society), and of sensuously experiencing something to which one felt one was entitled. Nature, as a feminized, healing, and nurturing force, worked well as a cultural accoutrement to the symbolic furnishing of this space.

Enter the stranger

Of course, capitalism was and remains a formidable desiring machine. The monetary flux, the means of production, of manpower, of new markets, all that is the flow of desire. It's enough to consider the sum of contingencies at the origin of capitalism to see to what degree it has been a crossroads of desires, and that its infrastructure, even its economy, was inseparable from the phenomena of desire. (Guattari 1995: 63)

Yet again this brings us back to the question of what is hospitality, and what are the processes behind the production of hospitable space today? In order to approach these questions I would like to quote Derrida one last time, at some length, as he contemplates the arrival of the stranger who one has been waiting for and expecting – a stranger who is greeted by the master of the household with the following words:

Nature as an esthetic object which is packaged and explained via the Eastern philosophy of Feng-Shui, and which is expected to instill a sense of calm, stillness, and well-being upon spa visitors. Photo: Tom O'Dell.

'Enter quickly,' quickly, in other words, without delay and without waiting. Desire is waiting for what does not wait. The quest must make haste. Desire measures time since its abolition in the stranger's entering movement: the stranger, here the awaited guest, is not only someone to whom you say 'come,' but 'enter,' enter without waiting, make a pause in our home without waiting, hurry up and come in, 'come inside,' 'come within me,' not only toward me, but within me: occupy me, take place in me, which means, by the same token, also take my place, don't content yourself with coming to meet me, which means by the same token, also take my place, don't content yourself with coming to meet me or 'into my home'. Crossing the threshold is entering and not only approaching or coming. Strange logic, but so enlightening for us, that of an impatient master awaiting his guest as a liberator, his emancipator. It is *as if* the stranger or foreigner held the keys. This is always the situation of the foreigner, in politics too, that of coming as a legislator to lay down the law and liberate the people or the nation by coming from outside, by entering into the nation of the house, into the

home that lets him enter after having appealed to him. It's *as if* …
as if, then, the stranger could save the master and liberate the power
of his host; it's *as if* the master, *qua* master, were prisoner of his
subjectivity (his subjectivity is hostage). So it is indeed the master,
the one who invites, the inviting host, who becomes the hostage
– and who really always has been … The guest (*hôte*) becomes the
host (*hôte*) of the host (*hôte*). (2000: 123 ff.)

In a context of absolute hospitality, the strangest foreigner one could
possibly imagine – whose very world-view could not be imaginable
in a context of absolute hospitality – would have to be 'the market' and the processes of commodification in which it is clothed.
How could one imagine a guest whose existence would make the
preconditions of your very existence (the preconditions of absolute
hospitality) impossible? But as Derrida points out, hospitality is a
highly ambivalent phenomenon. Absolute hospitality was never
able to close its doors, or turn its back to anyone. Not even the
market. For better or worse, we increasingly find ourselves living
in a cultural economy in which the market has long since ceased to
be a stranger: and is increasingly our host.

As our interest (and the interests of marketers, politicians, and
social planners) is increasingly directed towards the processes at work
in the new structure of attention, we find ourselves in a position
of having to (and at times wanting to) open ourselves to market
processes and the possibilities that these processes may have in
store for us. The possibility of happiness, contentment, well-being.
The possibility of being cared for and loved. But as we open our
homes and ourselves to these processes, we run the risk of finding
not just what we are looking for, but also a world of ambivalences.
The hospitable space of the bathroom will undoubtedly be able to
provide comfort, excitement, and a world of sensuous possibilities on many an occasion. But what will we be required to do in
the future to renew the magical potential of the bathroom, when
mould has begun to gather in the corners and the beige floor-tiles
feel so old-fashioned, so 2010? And finally, as we learn to associate
the sensation of well-being with the commoditized products and
services of the market, how will this affect the manner in which we
come to expect to be served by others in the name of wellness in the

future, when burning candles, incense, and warm baths have become blasé, if an intensified inward focus upon our own emotions further inhibits our ability to recognize the efforts and sacrifices of others?

The search for wellness, relaxation, and serenity is to some extent predicated upon our continued commitment to the world of work; to the commitment of our own work and the intensified commitment of the work of others, those we pay to pamper us and reward us. But it is also predicated upon a commitment to our own desires. As Felix Guattari argues in the opening quote of this section, capitalism has a strong propensity to take on the characteristics of a 'desiring machine' (Guattari 1995: 63), but as he and Deleuze point out elsewhere (Deleuze & Guattari 2004: 28), it is not a machine that simply prompts abstract wants or facilitates ephemeral dreams. Its products are quite real, affecting people and having consequences for people's daily lives in different ways, in different contexts and times (Guattari 1995: 54). This is an important insight to bear in mind as one reflects upon the phenomenon of conditional hospitality in relation to the spa's arrival in the home.

Spas have always been sites in which people have focused their desires and allowed them to find expression. The spas of the eighteenth and nineteenth centuries promoted themselves as spaces of medical activity and physical healing, and the hope of curing oneself of any of a wide array of ailments was a part of their appeal. The services and forms of hospitality which they provided toward this goal could include everyone from the Swedish king and royal family to the most destitute members of local society. But the search for better physical health was only a small part of the spa's appeal and never sufficiently strong in itself to last long as its economic basis.

For economic feasibility, spas always had to rely on their reputations as summer destinations. To this end, they functioned as places in which the well-to-do could entertain themselves, play, relax, and socialize in ways that were never possible in the usual context of daily life in high society. This was a world of romantic possibilities and potential career opportunities that kindled the imagination. But spas worked in this regard because they offered patrons the opportunity to walk about in parks, to socialize in reading rooms, and to 'accidentally' bump into one another at meal times. As a culturally contextualized space of conditional hospitality, spas specialized in the provisioning of opportunities for guests to meet guests.

In the eighteenth century, the presence of destitute peasants could easily be accepted by the aristocracy since there was never the remotest chance that these two groups of patrons could be confused. The upper classes could acknowledge the presence of others and move on past them. The situation became more complicated over the course of the nineteenth century as new groups of middle-class patrons were increasingly drawn to the spas. In response spa-owners became increasingly adept at designing different packages of incremental hospitality. Spas were still popular as meeting places, but now the meeting grounds were divided into first- and second-class facilities and treatments. In other words, spas learned to fine-tune the manner in which they could offer hospitality in increments – socially, culturally, and medically – and the entire process was facilitated by their ability to keep these different groups of guests moving in close proximity to one another, but nonetheless in slightly different circles.

The spas working in the decades at the turn of this century operate in a very different context. The cultural context was in part marked by the retreat of the welfare state and rise of neo-liberal ideas and philosophies in which people were increasingly urged to fend for themselves, and 'invest' in themselves. It was a context in which Swedes increasingly viewed their health as being threatened by the stresses of work specifically, and life in general. The desire to get away from it all, to experience something new, and to find new sources of strength and energy, replaced previous desires for collective forms of vacationing in which one could meet new people and make new friends. In this regard, the hospitality of the spa was increasingly directed toward the individual and her/his personal experience, but it would be incorrect to portray them as spaces of pure hyper-individualism. Few spa patrons attended spas on their own. On the contrary, these were facilities that specialized in forms of intimate hospitality that brought couples and small groups of friends together for shorter periods of time ranging from a few hours to a few days.

However, in order to succeed spas had to re-invent themselves and their cultural trappings in ways that would once again pique the imagination of the upper and middle classes. In the new millennium, the esthetics and architecture of the facilities have been carefully planned and implemented to do this by creating specific types of atmosphere and emotional impact. But in a context in which we are speaking of a cultural economy, it is important to bear in mind that spas deliver more than carefully planned esthetic packages. They also mobilize signs, symbols, and representations of health, calm, and harmony to impact upon the body. These were not just signs that were read by the eye, for in the form of such things as New Age music, burning incense, warm baths, and terry cloth robes they were felt and perceived by the body and senses.

As a further extension of this cultural work, spas provide guests with the opportunity to engage in, and experiment with embodied forms of Eastern philosophies including yoga, meditation, Tai Chi and Qigong. In so doing, they draw the realm of the spiritual into the market context of the services they provide. This, however, is not a pious finger-pointing form of spirituality, but rather one which patrons can choose to embrace, tentatively experiment with, or ultimately hold at a distance. In this way, in contrast to the health farms of the late twentieth century which specialized in strict diets and alcohol-free traditions, spas are places in which one can strive toward a state of better well-being while having fun and trying something new. They are playgrounds for people with the means to afford them, but they are shrouded in an aura of serious play implicitly understood as preventative care. The juxtapositioning of the spa with the realm of the spiritual contributes to this aura.

Equally important, however, is the manner in which perceptions of wellness are evoked through the small ritualistic practices of both spa personnel and guests. Guests do not just receive massages or treatments. They are forever being led into rooms in which these activities are repeatedly performed, according to carefully scripted choreographies of their own. And in other areas of the spa, guests themselves often engage in the rites of wellness with little reflection – lowering their voices, touching one another, and performing small favors for each other. In this sense, rituals can be understood as one of the most important commodities that spas sell: the rituals – and ritualized context – of wellness.

Much of what is at issue here is concerned with the production of the ephemeral – defined in terms of atmosphere, spirituality, fun, harmony, and well-being. But as Deleuze and Guattari point out, desires, and the efforts to meet desires, have real consequences (2004: 28). There is more at stake here than esthetics, and the circulation of signs and representations in promotional materials. Spas of the nineteenth century turned out to be extraordinarily capable 'social machines', efficiently working to separate categories of patrons while simultaneously also creating ample circumstances (and arenas of interaction) in which it was possible to make new acquaintances and develop new forms of social relations amongst patrons of similar standing. In this sense, they were sites of medical investigation, health care, recreation, and relaxation, but they were also particularly adept in the techniques of reproducing class.

In the 2000s the spa phenomenon has given new life to the hotel industry. In this context people do not come for weeks on end, but find a new focus for weekend get-a-ways, and midweek interludes. As these facilities grew in popularity, they provided employment opportunities for a new cadre of young female care-providers. Many of these women have hopes, dreams, and desires of their own: of helping people, of starting their own businesses, and of getting to know their patrons and thereby providing them with better services. The rigors of work in a large spa, however, can also snuff such dreams, or put them on hold. These, ultimately, are some of the limits, potentials, and consequences of conditional hospitality in the cultural economy of the new millennium.

The linkage between the home and the spa is in many ways a linkage of desires, but as I have argued here, these are not desires that necessarily flow in a unidirectional manner from the spa to the home or vice versa. They are part of a larger bifurcated network of values, hopes, fears, and ideals in society at large – drawing at times on Eastern philosophies, at times on Western concerns (over burnout and stress, for example), connected in inconspicuous ways to images of nature as a healing force, and often linked to the realities of everyday life, family, and work.

The bathroom is interesting in this context because it reminds us that the cultural economy is not a phenomenon limited to the public world of business and work. It is intimately entwined with our private lives and the activities we engage in within the four walls of our homes. The offering of hospitality has been part and parcel of this process ever since the first door was opened to the first stranger in need, although as the obligation of hospitality has been commodified through the centuries, it has increasingly come to be understood as a metaphorical relationship. In this regard, the phenomenon of hospitality and the journey it has taken through the market serves to remind us of the depths to which we can trace the processes that we now refer to in terms of the cultural economy. This is not necessarily a new phenomenon.

But as the spa has come home, it has gone from being a site of social interaction to one of social disjuncture and self-reflection. This 'space for myself' is a hospitable space earned for services rendered (a gift of sorts), but whereas the hospitality of the commercial spa relies on the services of others, the bathroom is a space of self-service in which one's own well-being is dependent upon one's own ability to create the time and pre-conditions for relaxation (cf. Fredriksson 2006: 33). And while hospitality always implies a relationship between guests and hosts, this is a space that only necessitates a relationship with the offerings of the market. Paradoxically, as a consequence of this, it could be argued that while the objective was to convert the bathroom into a hospitable space for oneself, it was at best a hospitable space without hospitality – one without the services or welcoming of the host, of the Other. Or perhaps if seen in another perspective, it could be argued that the market has worked well to host our desires, accommodate them, and nurture them. Once again, this links certain avenues of our well-being to the labor we perform to earn our incomes and participate in the market. In this context, productivity is a prerequisite of our ability to access these particular offerings of well-being: work is the means to the relaxation and rejuvenation that we seek as a reaction to the tempo and conditions of work (and daily life in general). This is the market's hostile gesture towards us, even as we appeal to it in our attempts to create and find new hospitable spaces for ourselves. But as Derrida has pointed out, hostility and hospitality always go hand in hand, threatening each other as they do so.

However, all is not negative. The bathroom has proven to be a highly flexible laboratory for sensory experimentation and training; a laboratory in which Swedes have enthusiastically and reflectively experimented with the effects a scented candle, a little bath-oil, or new floor-tiles could have upon them. In this sense, the market has proven highly capable of working magic and of delivering on many of the promises it has made. But what I have tried to demonstrate here is that this always has consequences. It raises the question of whose interests are being served, whose interests are being overlooked, and how might we unwittingly be implicated in all of this?

In order to make us feel relaxed and pampered, spas have to work vigorously in the space of the pre-reflexive gap. And to be most successful they have to do so in ways in which we are not fully aware. To the extent that we end up feeling better, we can perhaps be glad that they have learned to achieve so much in such a small space of time and body. But as other actors, some perhaps with political agendas quite different from our own, learn to work just as effectively in the half-second delay, how long or to what extent will we be willing to turn a blind eye? And what types of new competencies will we need to learn to shore up a line of defense in the moment before consciousness? These are all questions we shall have to face in the future. And in fact, in light of the degree to which our senses are already being targeted by others who are striving to make an impression upon us, we should already be staring a number of them squarely in the face today.

Judging upon our current ability to work the new structure of attention to meet our own needs, there may be some reason for hope here. As we experiment with new ways of structuring our own emotions (and indeed school our children into this field of experimentation through the purchase of such toys as spa kits), we begin to open the doors of perception through which we can begin to discover and recognize the grammar of sensuous affect. But experimentation is not enough; an increased cognitive and corporeal awareness of the mechanisms at work in a cultural economy ever more focused upon our inner being is essential if we are to develop new dispositions of interpretation and understanding. The production of such an increased degree of awareness, in relation to a very specific portion of the leisure industry – spas and the longing for well-being – has been the primary ambition of this book.

Notes

1. Spas

1 Arndt, Palmeri & Arner, 2003: 42.

2 Press release published online <http://www.hotels-weekly.com>.

3 For summaries of these statistics, see <http://www.traveldailynews.com/makeof. asp?central_id=521&permanent_id=17>, <http://www.discoverspas.com/news/ newsevents114.shtml>, and <http://www.discoverspas.com/news/newsstudies7. shtml>.

4 These figures are based upon information obtained in interviews conducted with spa managers in which they discussed the growth of their own facilities. Unfortunately, reliable industry statistics are still not available in Sweden.

5 Clearly, there are exceptions to this tendency, from the classic work of MacCannell (1976) to more contemporary works such as Crouch (1999), and the criticisms of Franklin and Crang (2001: 6 ff.) toward the tourism literature. Unfortunately, the work of these scholars is not the mainstay of tourism studies. On the contrary, far too much of the work being done is focused on managerially oriented case-studies, branch analyses, and instrumental discussions of developing trends or problems in tourism. As Franklin and Crang (2001) point out, there is some work in the field of tourism that links it to more broadly defined social and cultural processes. But tourism studies still needs to take a more rigorous approach to its compartmentalization and its objects of study, and to demonstrate how tourism (and leisure) are integrated aspects of everyday life.

6 In addition to work I have published on tourism and the experience economy (see O'Dell & Billing 2005 and O'Dell 2007a, for example), the book in hand draws on a series of studies I have conducted that have used spas to problematize different aspects of the cultural economy (see, for example, O'Dell 2005b; 2007b; 2006). Sections from these texts appear in chapters two, three, and four of this book.

7 It should be noted that Pine and Gilmore wrote and published their works in the period of heated economic activity which at the time was referred to as the 'New Economy'. Many economists were busy trying to identify the next trend in economic development. The experience economy that Pine and Gilmore identified was only one of the potential new futures and trends which many management

theorists were anticipating. Other 'hot ideas' at the time included discussions of 'funky business' (Ridderstråle & Nordström 2002), 'serious play' (Schrage 1999), 'the dream society' (Jensen 1999) and 'the creative class' (Florida 2002). Unfortunately, while Pine and Gilmore wanted to define the coming of a new economic epoch, their work remained highly ahistorical. As the work of other scholars makes clear (see, for example, Cocks 2001; Hannigan 1998 & Peiss 1986), rather than representing a new phase of economic activity, the processes at work under the mantle of the experience economy can better be understood as an intensification of a long-existing interest in the realm of experiences than the sudden development of an entirely new and distinctive economic era.

8 For a more detailed discussion of the cultural, economic, and political consequences that the interest in experiences has had in Scandinavia, see Ek 2005; Hultman 2007; Löfgren 2005; O'Dell 2005a.

9 See Aungkasuvapala (2005); Bacon (1997); Mackaman (1998); Slyomovics (1993: 46 ff.).

2. Spas and the Shifting Context of Conditional Hospitality

1 The sheer number of market-related hits that the Internet instantly provides may to some extent say more about the Internet as a market-driven mode of interconnection than the manner in which most people first think about hospitality, but it does also reflect the prevalence with which hospitality has come to be perceived as a marketable commodity.

2 These key words are derived in part from the list of the first ten references provided by Google, <http://www.google.se/search?q=hospitality&hl=sv&lr=&start=0&sa=N>), s.v. 'hospitality', accessed on November 8, 2006; see also <http://www.hospitality-industry.com/>.

3 See *The New Shorter Oxford English Dictionary on Historical Principles* (1993: 1158 & 1266–67); *The Barnhart Dictionary of Etymology* (1988: 492).

4 It should be noted that the form of hospitality interrogated in this chapter is characterized by a situation in which the guest/host relationship is bound by commercialized processes of exchange. It is, in other words, a phenomenon limited and controlled by contextually defined laws that place obligations upon both the guest and the host. As a result, it never approaches the phenomenon that Derrida called 'absolute hospitality' (Derrida 2000: 83). Nonetheless, the immersion of the notion of hospitality in a discourse of exchange and market economics has had strong implications for the manner in which hospitality has been popularly perceived, consumed, produced, and spatially organized. The focus of analysis for this chapter lies, in other words, upon a very conditional context of hospitality, and it is the issue of conditionality (and its consequences) which I argue is in need of further interrogation.

5 From Hellman 1860: 16

6 See Weisz (2001) for a discussion of this in relation to the French context.

7 In the French context, Douglas Mackaman has noted that over half the spa guests

in the late nineteenth century were men (1998: 135 ff.). Here, social mobility seems to have been of significance, as the ability for a young man to make contact with other men of position in a leisure context was seen as a golden opportunity to secure the sort of future employment contacts that would facilitate one's ascent up the socio-economic ladder. In a similar manner, men of standing could entertain the hope of meeting other men whom they would have a use for outside of this temporary leisure setting. The situation was not radically different in Sweden, as men also took advantage of the situation here to further their political, economic, or social agendas (Lagerqvist 1978). A list of eminent guests, such as the one published by *Ramlösa Brunns- och Badtidning*, obviously played a role in nurturing these types of ambitions. In contrast to the French context, however, men were in the minority at Swedish spas, as it was usual for over 60 per cent of all guests in the late nineteenth century to be women (Mansén 2001: 62).

8 The King of Sweden himself contributed a larger endowment to Ramlösa, in 1826, that was to be used to help those without means.

9 See Strang (2004) for a discussion of the significance that has been attributed to water in a wider European context.

10 Most Swedish spas from the very beginning provided similar services that included hospital facilities and living quarters designated for the poor. These were usually financed through a combination of private donations and revenues generated by spa fees. In addition to these sources of income, most Swedish spas constructed elaborate systems of fining patrons for everything from arriving late for their cure, or napping during the day without permission, to a fine at one spa for departing guests who had failed to break any of the spa rules, and thereby had not supported the spa through the payment of any fines (Bergmark 1989: 20 ff.; Mansén 2001: 506 ff.). Revenues generated from these fines played an important role in subsidizing the hospital and other facilities for the poor.

11 The need to maintain a pleasant and harmonic atmosphere at the spa was so great that Dr Hellman explicitly instructed guests coming to Ronneby always to make the best of things and try to get along with the other guests, but when this was impossible, to simply stay away from people they found to be disagreeable (1860: 76).

12 See Derrida 1999 & 2000; and Dikeç 2002.

13 Industry-wide statistics do not exist at present. The figures presented here are based upon interviews I have conducted with spa managers, and reflect the situation at those specific resorts.

3. Magic, Ritual, and the Mass Production of Serenity

1 For stylistic reasons I will refer to these three places simply as Varberg Kurort, Varberg's Asia Spa, and Hasseludden.

2 See the discussion in the introduction to this book, as well as that in du Gay & Pryke (2002: 2 ff.) for a presentation and delineation of some of the ways in

which the metaphor of 'the cultural economy' can be understood. Since a larger part of the discussion in this book's introduction is dedicated to this topic, I will not labor the issue here.

3   As other cultural theorists have argued, much of the cultural phenomena associated with modernity have unfortunately often been aligned with processes of demystification and disenchantment. Increasingly, however, these and other scholars have questioned the accuracy of this academic (and popular) propensity to define magic and modernity as antagonistically opposed, and have insisted upon the need to reconsider the manner in which magic may still operate as an integral aspect of modernity. My intention here is to align myself with this perspective, and illustrate one way in which magic might be understood as a vitally integrated aspect of daily life in contemporary society. For further discussion and examples of other studies in this vein, see Berg, 2003; Löfgren & Willim, 2005; Meyer & Pels, 2003; Taussig, 1993; Thrift, 2000b.

4   Sensa SPA brochure (2003).

5   Mauss distinguishes between 'true magicians' and 'those charlatans who turn up at fairs, or Braham jugglers who brag to us about spirits. The magician pretends because pretence is demanded of him, because people seek him out and beseech him to act.' (2001: 118) The magician, in other words, is part of a larger cultural context in which the expectations of others work upon him. He is part of a system of knowledge, and he possesses portions of knowledge not accessible to the larger believing society, but he himself – despite his props, and conscious manipulation of them – believes in the power of the magic he wields and manipulates.

6   <http://www.hasseludden.com>, accessed on 2007-09-24.

7   Hasseludden's homepage explains that 'Yasuragi is … the name of our bathing facilities in which you can enjoy several different types of bathing pools – warm indoor springs, hot outdoor springs, and cooling swimming pools' (<http://www.hasseludden.com>, accessed on 2003-09-02).

8   In describing Hasseludden's original appearances, a manager at the facility claimed that up until the Yasuragi concept was developed in the 1990s, the place looked like any other bland municipal Swedish bathhouse from the early seventies. This was, in other words, a place that originally lacked any form of magical charm or aura.

9   Quoted from *Varbergs Kurort Hotell & Spa* brochure 2002: 46, my emphasis).

10 As Kevin Hetherington has noted, 'The viscous has a tendency to remain tacky – it does not always disappear completely in fact, it continues to tack. It has a motility as well as a mobility – it moves between a status of presence and absence and is transformed by so doing' (Hetherington 2002: 162). His discussion is primarily concerned with the role processes of disposal and absence play as an important aspect of consumption. In the case of Varberg Kurort, the spa has to partially 'rid itself' of aspects of its history – or at least tone them down. But at the same time, the spa is dependent upon the ability of this history to seep out of the walls of the facility, and fix itself to the experience of the spa's guests. My objective here is to extend Hetherington's line of argumentation. While he focuses upon processes of

disposal and 'secondhandedness' in relation to consumer goods, I am endeavoring to demonstrate how history and architecture can be worked in a similar manner to endow specific forms of meaning to the experiences of spa guests.

11 West Coast Spa is not the actual name of the other facility, but a name I have made up for purposes of anonymity.

12 See for example, *Varbergs Stadshotell & Asia Spa* brochure 2006: 17.

13 <http://www.yasuragi.se/info.asp/id/152516>, accessed on July 3, 2007.

14 <http://www.yasuragi.se/info.asp/id/152516>, accessed on July 3, 2007.

15 This representation of sun consumption is intimately linked with practices that many people in Sweden indulge in, and feel united with. The consumption of sunlight is, in this part of the world, an act that borders upon the religious, and more than tangentially touches upon beliefs of health and well-being.

16 <http://www.hasseludden.com>.

17 <http://www.hasseludden.com>, accessed on 2003-09-02.

18 These specific quotes are taken from Zernike (2005: 9) and Cereceda (2002: 49) respectively, but are representative of a few of the larger trends currently in vogue in the spa industry.

19 Varberg Kurort is unique in the Swedish context, for in addition to a large assortment of offerings of a recreational nature, such as weekend getaways, Sunday packages, golf packages, day passes, and wedding packages, the spa, as mentioned earlier, employs a wide range of therapists and healthcare personnel, and provides special care opportunities for cancer victims (and their families) as well as help for individuals with eating disorders. It is, in this sense, tightly bound with the established field of medical practice. However, it also offers more New Age-oriented activities such as Qigong and Tai Chi.

20 Bauman 1997 & 1998; Harvey 2000; Sennett 1999: 19 ff.; see also Castells (1997: 252 ff., and to a lesser extent 1996: 213) for a discussion of the manner in which the downsizing of the welfare state is linked to larger economic processes and competitiveness between nation-states.

21 Public discourse at the turn of the twenty-first century often portrayed burn-out as a nearly epidemic phenomenon in Sweden. Some estimates presented in the Swedish mass media in 2004 put the total number of people on sick leave due to burn-out in the hundreds of thousands (Friberg 2006: 20 ff.). And while it was not always clear who was on sick leave due to burn-out or for other reasons (and indeed one could debate what burn-out actually was, and how it was defined and identified), national statistics showed that the number of people on sick leave for more than a year increased from 75,000 individuals in 1997 to 120,000 in 2001 (Hammarlin 2008: 19). Against this background, burn-out was perceived by many as a real threat to their health and livelihood. Spas, as the managers I have spoken with have explained, actively positioned themselves to take advantage of this situation, and worked to establish themselves as places of respite and protection from burn-out.

22 Here, the will to believe may be stronger than the actual belief, as the belief in the

magical power of the spa always balances tenuously on the ability of the spa and its personnel to live up to the expectations of their clientele, while actual belief in the magic may be further weakened by the diverse needs and motives of its clientele. For many, a visit to a spa may merely be a fun way of pampering oneself, no more spiritual in nature than a trip to the pub. For others, the visit might be laced to a greater extent with the ambiguous feeling of 'I don't know if this will help me feel better, but at this point it can't hurt', with desperation playing a greater role than any actual belief. Nonetheless, amongst at least some people whom I have spoken with, a visit to a spa is linked to a real belief that it will help them feel better, and it is this aspect of the spa visit that can play a central role in the magic of the experience.

4. Spa Sensibilities

1   It should be noted that this undated Varberg brochure was published after the 2002 brochure cited elsewhere in this volume, most likely in 2004.

2   I shall be referring to three slightly different but related terms: affect, emotion, and feelings. Although closely related, these terms are not fully interchangeable. My thinking here, and the manner in which I shall invoke these terms, is heavily influenced by the work of Antonio Damasio (2003) and Nigel Thrift (2004). Following Damasio, I see feelings as being generated out of emotions. Emotions move us, causing facial expressions (the curling of the lips into a smile, the wrinkling of eyebrows into a frown), bodily reactions (the falling of tears, production of perspiration), and a mobile physical relationship to the world (through fight and flight reactions, for example). Emotions are in this sense 'public' events, while feelings are 'private' (Damasio 2003: 27). Feelings 'are always hidden, like all mental images necessarily are, unseen to anyone other than their rightful owner, the most private property of the organism in whose brain they occur' (ibid.: 28). In this sense, emotions are more closely linked to the body, while feelings have a larger home in the mind. But they are not entirely separate, since feelings could not have a home anywhere if it were not for the emotional reactions of the body. Affect is of a larger order, encompassing body and mind; it is a kind of intelligence, a way of knowing the world (Thrift 2004: 60).

3   The name presented here is fictive for the purpose of anonymity.

4   The preconditions for movement established by the *yukata* may be even more apparent for people, such as myself, not accustomed to wearing robes or tight-fitting dresses. In this sense, issues of gender and previous experiences of mobility may work to heighten or diminish the perceptions facilitated by the *yukata*.

5   That said, it should be noted that impressions of audio-immobility are fragile. They are constantly destabilized by forms of micro-mobilities built into the textures of the music that is used to create a sense of serenity and stillness. This includes everything from the very rhythm of the music and the subtlest of stereo effects it may include, to such phenomena as the sounds of running water, rain, and wind that can accompany many New Age recordings. The sensations

created in the treatment room may be described in terms of calmness, serenity, or a slowing of time, and these are sensations that may be partially reinforced by processes of audio-immobility, but it must be pointed out that they are also achieved through the subtle (and not so subtle) invocations of different forms of mobility.

6   The power of touch to heal, sooth, and diminish stress is a frequently made claim in the world of spas and one that has increasingly gained repute in the mass media (see Kantor 2004; Nordgren 2004; Strandberg 2004). The degree to which this may or may not be true is still debated within the medical community (Taylor 2001: 35).

7   In the course of my observations, I never saw any form of activity that was overtly sexual, and in all my conversations with spa-goers I have only heard one story in which sexuality came into play. In that case it was related to a young couple in their mid-twenties who were seen necking in a hot tub. The person relating the story to me found the behavior to be somewhat odd and out of place, and explained it partly by referring to the couple's young age, and the fact that they cannot have understood that this was inappropriate behavior at a spa. Sexuality, in other words, may not be completely absent from the types of spas I am describing here, but it is culturally defined as out of place and inappropriate. Intimacy, closeness, and the ability of the spa to bring people together have clear limits (at least in the public areas of the spa) which most spa-goers seem to be acutely in tune with.

8   Obviously, there are people in the background of the spa employed to clean the facility or care for the technical equipment in the spa, and these people are always moving about, but the bulk of most spas' personnel rosters are composed of therapists, masseuses, and other care providers who are assigned a specific station in and around which they perform their work.

9   The name of this spa has been changed here for reasons of anonymity.

10 *Webster's New World Dictionary* defines kinaesthesis as 'the sensation of position, movement, tension, etc. of parts of the body, perceived through nerve end organs in muscles, tendons and joints' (1986: 776).

11 The processes involved here might be likened (perhaps not coincidentally) to the processes of turning your enemy's powers against her/him, which Weiner (2003: 148: ff.) has argued is an integral aspect of the working of magic in some contexts.

12 A twenty-four hour stay at a Swedish spa begins at approximately $200, while a basic week-long stay starts at $1,100. Guests purchasing extra treatments and products quickly find themselves paying significantly larger sums. By and large, Swedish spas attract middle- and upper-class patrons. Varberg Kurort, it should be pointed out, is something of an exception. While Varberg Kurort does attract its share of middle- and upper-class guests, as I have already noted previously it still has a medical function, and thus includes categories of patients whose costs can be covered to varying extents by governmental or other institutions.

13 My point is reinforced by recent findings in the neurosciences which point to the significant role that bodily movement plays as an anchor for feelings (see Damasio

(2003) for a general discussion of this research); see also Smith (2007) for a more phenomenologically based analysis of the link between bodily practices and states of mind as related to Ashtanga Vinyasa Yoga; and Thrift (2000: 44) for a discussion of the magical effects repetitive 'performative technologies' can have in the shaping of emotional energies.

5. Bringing the Spa Home

1 <http://www.amazon.com/Scientific-Explorers-Spa-Science-Chemistry/dp/ B0006OHMU6/ref=pd_sim_t_title_1>, accessed on February 22, 2008, original spelling.

2 Quoted from an Aquapool advertisement printed in *Sköna hem* (1989 2: 147).

3 <http://www.viivvilla.se/41857.aspx>, accessed on February 25, 2008.

4 See for example Fürst 2006: 86; Hed 2006: 132 ff.

5 See Shove 2003: 104 for a discussion of the manner in which similar processes unfolded in the English context.

6 Cecila Fredriksson (2006) has likened this space to a 'machine of enjoyment' run by 'mood creators'. Yet as she points out, it is a space with strings attached, since 'creating the right mood' often requires a great deal of domestic work. In order to create an atmosphere of purity and harmony similar to that associated with commercial spas, the home bathroom has to undergo a great deal of cleaning, ordering, and rearranging. And in the home, it is often the woman who is planning to relax who has to do this work before she embarks on the endeavor to find new harmony and balance.

7 International statistics published by the International Spa Association in 2004 demonstrated that 23 per cent of all spa visits were conducted by men (<http://www.traveldailynews.com/makeof.asp?central_id=521&permanent_id=17>). National statistics for Swedish spas do not exist, unfortunately. The impression which I developed over the course of my fieldwork in spas (between 2002 and 2007), which is shared by the spa managers with whom I have spoken, was that the clientele of the Swedish spas became increasingly heterogeneous over that period. In 2002 most of the people I observed at spas were between forty-five and seventy years old, the vast majority of them being women – either mothers and daughters, or two friends out to enjoy themselves. Perhaps 20–25 per cent of visitors were men, almost always accompanied by their wives. Today it is not uncommon to find young couples in their twenties visiting spas, although the majority of visitors are over thirty. In this sense the average age of the spa visitor seems to have dropped slightly. Men seem to constitute about 40 per cent of all visitors (still accompanied by their wives or partners). According to one spa manager, the split between men and women is almost even on the weekends, while women constitute a slightly larger percentage of spa visitors during the week.

References

Published sources

Airey, David & Tribe, John (2000) 'Education for Hospitality'. In Conrad Lashley & Alison Morrison (eds.), *In Search of Hospitality: Theoretical Perspectives and Debates*, pp. 276–292. Oxford: Butterworth-Heinemann.

Amin, Ash & Thrift, Nigel (2007) 'Cultural-economy and cities', *Progress in Human Geography* 31(2): pp. 143–161.

Arndt, Michael, Palmeri, Christopher & Arner, Faith (2003) '"Dog Days" Journey into Night: Rain, job jitters … Americans are forgoing vacations in droves', *BusinessWeek* August 25: p. 42.

Aronsson, Lars (2007) 'Kartor over kulturella ekonomier'. In Lars Aronsson, Jonas Bjä-lesjö, and Susanne Johansson (eds.), *Kulturell ekonomi: Skapandet av värden, platser och identiteter I upplevelsesamhället*, pp. 15–39. Lund: Studentlitteratur.

Aquapool advertisement (1989) *Sköna hem* 2: p. 147.

Attfield, Judy (2000) *Wild Things: The Material Culture of Everyday Life*. Oxford: Berg.

Aungkasuvapala, Narongsakdi (2005) *Health Tourism – The Rising Star: Strategies for Success*. Published online <http://www.tatnews.org/emagazine/1983.asp>, accessed on May 31, 2005.

Bacon, William (1997) 'The rise of the German and the demise of the English spa industry: a critical analysis of business success and failure', *Leisure Studies* 16: pp. 173–187.

Bahco sauna advertisement (1968). 'Mysiga klubben', *Allt i Hemmet* 4: p. 12.

Barnhart Dictionary of Etymology (1988) Robert K. Barnhart (ed.), New York: The H. W. Wilson Company.

Bauman, Zygmunt (1997) *Postmodernity and its Discontents*. Cambridge: Polity Press.

Bauman, Zygmunt (1998) *Globalization: The Human Consequences*. New York: Columbia University Press.

Bauman, Zygmunt (2000) *Liquid Modernity*. Oxford: Blackwell Publishers.

Berg, Per Olof (2003) 'Magic in Action: Strategic Management in a New Economy'. In Barbara Czarniawska & Guje Sevón (eds.), *The Northern Lights: Organization Theory in Scandinavia*. Copenhagen: Copenhagen Business School Press.

Bergmark, Matts (1985) *Bad och Bot: Om vattnet som läkemedel och njutningsmedel*. Stockholm: Prisma Magnum.

Better Homes and Gardens (2003) Special issue MindBodySpirit.

Bogard, William (2000) 'Smoothing Machines and the Constitution of Society', *Cultural Studies*, 14(2): pp. 269–294.

Bowen, John & Ford, Robert (2004) 'What Experts Say about Managing Hospitality Service Delivery Systems', *International Journal of Contemporary Hospitality Management* 16(1): pp. 394–401.

Brink, Johanna (undated) 'Återerövring av en gammal japansk idé'. In Kerstin Kåll (ed.), *Yasuragi: Stillhet, skönhet, harmoni*, pp. 152–159. Stockholm: Bokförlaget Fischer & Co.

Broomé, Elisabeth (2006) 'Från undanskymd vrå till hemma-spa, badrummet under

50 år'. Published online <http://www.viivilla.se/badrum/fran-undanskymd-vra-till-hemma-spa-badrummet-under-50-ar.aspx>, accessed March 18, 2008.

Brotherton, Bob (1999) 'Towards a definitive view of the nature of hospitality and hospitality management', *International Journal of Contemporary Hospitality Management*. 11: 4: pp. 165–173.

Campbell, Collin (1999) 'The Easternisation of the West'. In Bryan Wilson & Jamie Cresswell (eds.), *New Religious Movements: Challenge and Response*, pp. 35–48. London: Routledge.

Castells, Manuel (1996) *The Rise of the Network Society*. Malden: Blackwell Publishers.

Castells, Manuel (1997) *The Power of Identity*. Malden: Blackwell Publishers.

Cereceda, Johan (2002) 'Magisk sjöbotten läker ömma leder', *Spa Magazine* 2: pp. 49–50.

Christersdotter, Maria (2005) 'Mobile Dreams'. In Tom O'Dell (ed.), *Experiencescapes: Tourism, Culture, and Economy*, pp. 91–109. Copenhagen: Copenhagen Business School Press.

Cocks, Catherine (2001) *Doing the Town: The Rise of Urban Tourism in the United States, 1850–1915*. Berkeley: University of California Press.

Crouch, David (1999) *Leisure/Tourism Geographies: Practices and Geographical Knowledge*. London: Routledge.

Damasio, Antonio (2003) *Looking for Spinoza: Joy, Sorrow, and the Feeling Brain*. Orlando: Harcourt, Inc.

Deal, Terrence & Kennedy, Allan (2000) *Corporate Cultures: The Rites and Rituals of Corporate Life*. Reading: Perseus Publishing.

Deleuze, Gilles (1988) *Spinoza: Practical Philosophy*. San Francisco: City Light Books.

Deleuze, Gilles & Guattari, Félix (1987) *A Thousand Plateaus: Capitalism and Schizophrenia*. Minneapolis: University of Minnesota Press.

Deleuze, Gilles & Guattari, Felix (2004) *Anti-Oedipus*. London: Continuum.

Derrida, Jacques (1999) *Adieu To Emmanuel Levinas*. Stanford: Stanford University Press.

Derrida, Jacques (2000) *Of Hospitality*. Stanford: Stanford University Press.

Dikeç, Mustafa (2002) 'Pera Peras Poros: Longing for Spaces of Hospitality', *Theory, Culture & Society* 19(1–2), pp. 227–247.

du Gay, Paul & Pryke, Michael (2002) 'Cultural economy: An introduction'. In Paul du Gay & Michael Pryke (eds.), *Cultural Economy*, pp. 1–20. London: Sage.

Durkheim, Émile (2001) *The Elementary Forms of Religious Life*. Oxford: Oxford University Press.

Dyer, Richard (1997) *White*. London: Routledge.

Ek, Richard (2005) 'Regional Experiencescapes as Geo-economic Ammunition'. In Tom O'Dell & Peter Billing (eds.), *Experiencescapes: Tourism, Culture, and Economy*, pp. 69–89. Copenhagen: Copenhagen Business School Press.

Featherstone, Mike (2002) 'Cosmopolis: An Introduction'. *Theory Culture & Society*. 19(1–2): pp. 1–16.

Feld, Steven (2005) 'Places Sensed, Senses Placed: Toward a Sensuous Epistemology of Environments'. In David Howe (ed.), *Empire of the Senses: The Sensual Cultural Reader*, pp. 179–191. Oxford: Berg.

Firth, David & Carayol, Rene (2002) *My Voodoo: A Practical Guide to Unleashing the Magic in You and Your Work*. Oxford: Capstone.

Florida, Richard (2002) *The Rise of the Creative Class: And How It's Transforming Work, Leisure, Community and Everyday Life*. New York: Basic Books.

Foucault, Michel (1978) *The History of Sexuality: Volume 1, an Introduction*. New York: Penguin Books.

Franklin, Adrian & Crang, Mike (2001) 'The Trouble with Tourism and Travel Theory', *Tourist Studies* 1(1): pp. 5–22.

Fredriksson, Cecilia (2006) 'Hemma-spa – njutningsmaskin och stämningskreator'. In Robert Willim (ed.), *ETN: Hem*, pp. 25–36. Lund: Etnologiska Institutionen.

Friberg, Torbjörn (2006) *Diagnosing Burn-out: An Anthropological Study of a Social Concept in Sweden.* Lund: Lund University.

Frykman, Jonas (2004) 'I hetluften: Svensk bastu som ideologi och praktik'. In Christina Westergren (ed.), *Tio tvättar sig*, pp. 87–108. Stockholm: Nordiska museets förlag.

Fürst, Camilla (2006) 'Familjen fick ett relaxrum med guldkant', *Allt i Hemmet* 11: pp. 84–87.

Gartman, David (1994) *Auto Opium: A Social History of American Automobile Design.* London: Routledge.

Germann Molz, Jennie & Gibson, Sarah (2007) 'Introduction: Mobilizing and Mooring Hospitality'. In Jennie Germann Molz & Sarah Gibson (eds.), *Mobilizing Hospitality: The Ethics of Social Relations in a Mobile World*, pp. 1–25. Hampshire: Ashgate Publishing Limited.

Goffman, Erving (1971) *Relations in Public: Microstudies of the Public Order.* New York: Basic Books.

Goldschmidt Salomon, Karen Lisa (2005) 'Possessed by Enterprise: Values and Value-creation in Mandrake Management'. In Orvar Löfgren & Robert Willim (eds.), *Magic, Culture and The New Economy*, pp. 47–56. Oxford: Berg.

Greenwood, Susan (2000) *Magic, Witchcraft and the Otherworld*, Oxford: Berg.

Greenwood, Susan (2005) *The Nature of Magic: An Anthropology of Consciousness.* Oxford: Berg.

Guattari, Felix (1995) *Chaosophy.* New York: Semotext(e).

Gustavsberg advertisement (1988) *Allt i Hemmet* 4: pp. 39–42.

Hacking, Ian (1998) *Mad Travelers: Reflections on the Reality of Transient Mental Illnesses.* Charlottesville: University Press of Virginia.

Hall, Edward, T. (1990) *The Hidden Dimension.* New York: Anchor Books.

Hammarlin, Mia-Marie (2008) *Att leva som utbränd: En etnologisk studie av långtids-sjukskrivna.* Stehag: Brutus Östlings Bokförlag Symposion.

Hannerz, Ulf (1992) *Cultural Complexity: Studies in the Social Organization of Meaning.* New York: Columbia University Press.

Hannigan, John (1998) *Fantasy City: Pleasure and Profit in the Postmodern Metropolis.* London: Routledge.

Harvey, David (2000) *Spaces of Hope.* Berkeley: University of Berkeley Press.

Heal, Felicity (1990) *Hospitality in Early Modern England.* Oxford: Clarendon Press.

Heal, Felicity (1984) 'The Idea of Hospitality in Early Modern England'. *Past and Present.* 102: pp. 66–93.

Hed, Pernilla (2006) 'Badrum för umgänge', *Sköna hem* 11: pp. 132–133.

Heelas, Paul (1996) *The New Age Movement: The Celebration of Self and the Sacralization of Modernity.* Malden: Blackwell.

Heelas, Paul (1999) 'Prosperity and the New Age Movement: The Efficacy of Spiritual Economics'. In Bryan Wilson & Jamie Creswell (eds.), *New Religious Movements: Challenge and Response*, pp. 51–77. London: Routledge.

Heelas, Paul (2002) 'Work ethics, soft capitalism and the "turn to life"'. In Paul du Gay & Michael Pryke (eds.), *Cultural Economy: Cultural Analysis and Commercial Life*, pp. 78–96. London: Sage.

Hellman, A.F. (1860) *Ronneby: Dess Helsokällor och Bad m.m. En handbok för brunnssö-*

kande. Stockholm: Hörbergska Boktryckeriet. Published online <http://www.ronneby. se/PageUpload/7402/handbok.pdf>, accessed on March 25, 2008.

Hetherington, Kevin (2004) 'Secondhandedness: consumption, disposal, and absent presence', *Environment and Planning D: Society and Space* 22: pp. 157–173.

Hochschild, Arlie Russell (2003) *The Commercialization of Intimate Life: Notes from Home and Work*. Berkeley: University of California Press.

Howe, David (2005a) 'HYPERESTHESIA, or The Sensual Logic of Late Capitalism'. In David Howe (ed.), *Empire of the Senses: The Sensual Cultural Reader*, pp. 281–303. Oxford: Berg.

Howe, David (2005b) 'Introduction: Empire of the Senses'. In David Howe (ed.) *Empire of the Senses: The Sensual Cultural Reader*, pp. 1–20. Oxford: Berg.

Hultman, Johan (2007) 'Through the Protocol: Culture, Magic and GIS in the Creation of Regional Attractiveness', *Tourism Geographies* 9(3): pp. 318–336.

Hutchinson, Nichola (2006) 'Disabling Beliefs? Impaired Embodiment in the Religious Tradition of the West', *Body & Society* 12(4): pp. 1–23.

Icelandair advertisement (2002) 'The Icelandic Spa Cocktail', *Spa Magazine* 1: p. 40.

Jensen, Rolf (1999) *The Dream Society: How the Coming Shift from Information to Imagination Will Transform Your Business*. New York: McGraw-Hill.

Kantor, Jan (2004) 'Positiv närhet förutsätter jämlikhet', *Dagens Nyheter* Insidan, March 30: p. 10.

Kellner, Christina (2003) 'Friskvård gör anställda sjuka', *Svensk hotellrevy* 6–7: p. 22.

King, Carol (1995) 'What Is Hospitality?', *International Journal of Hospitality Management* 14 (3–4): pp. 219–234.

Klinkmann, Sven-Erik (2005) 'Cultural Kinesthesis in Mediascapes', *Ethnologia Scandinavica* 35: pp. 7–20.

Lagerqvist, Lars (1978) *Medevi Brunn 300 år 1678–1978*. Medevi: Medevi Brunn.

Lakoff, George & Johnson, Mark (1999) *Philosophy in the Flesh: The Embodied Mind and its Challenge to Western Thought*. New York: Basic Books.

Lasansky, Medina (2004) 'Introduction'. In Medina Lasansky & Brian McLaren (eds.), *Architecture and Tourism: Perception, Performance and Place*, pp. 1–14. Oxford: Berg.

Lash, Scott & Urry, John (1994) *Economies of Signs and Space*. London: Sage.

Lefebvre, Henri (1991) *The Production of Space*. Malden: Blackwell.

Levertin, Alfred (1990) *Varbergs hafskuranstalt: en kortare monografisk skildring*. Varberg: Cal-förlaget.

Lindblad, A. (1907) *Ramlösa Brunn 1707–1907*. Stockholm: Hasse W. Tullbergs Boktryckeri.

Lutz, Catherine (1998) *Unnatural Emotions: Everyday Sentiments on a Micronesian Atoll*. Chicago: University of Chicago Press.

Löfgren, Orvar (1989) 'Längtan till Landet Annorlunda'. In Bengt Sahlberg & Lars Vidén (eds.) *Längtan till Landet Annorlunda*, pp. 9–49. Stockholm: Gidlunds Bokförlag.

Löfgren, Orvar (1999) *On Holiday. A History of Vacationing*. Berkeley: University of California Press.

Löfgren, Orvar (2005) 'Cultural Alchemy: Translating the Experience Economy Into Scandinavian'. In Barbara Czarniawska & Guje Sevòn (eds.), *Global Ideas*. Malmö: Liber.

Löfgren, Orvar & Ehn, Billy. (2007) *När inget särskilt händer*. Stehag: Brutus Östlings Bokförlag Symposion.

Löfgren, Orvar & Willim, Robert (2005) *Magic, Culture and The New Economy*. Oxford: Berg.

MacCannell, Dean. 1976. *The Tourist: A New Theory of the Leisure Class*. London: MacMillan.

Mackaman, Douglas Peter (1998) *Leisure Settings: Bourgeois Culture, Medicine, and the Spa in Modern France*. Chicago: University of Chicago Press.

Mansén, Elisabeth (2001) *Ett paradis på jorden*. Stockholm: Atlantis.

Mansén, Elisabeth (2005) 'Brunnsliv & Kurortskultur I Ronneby 1705–2005'. In Lisa Hogdal (ed.), *Ronneby Brunn under trehundra år 1705–2005*, pp. 17–82. Stockholm: Byförlaget.

Mauss, Marcel. (1990) *The Gift*. New York: W. W. Norton.

Mauss, Marcel (2001) *A General Theory of Magic*. London: Routledge.

McFall, Liz (2002) 'Advertising, Persuasion and the Culture/Economy Dualism'. In Paul du Gay & Michael Pryke (eds.), *Cultural Economy: Cultural Analysis and Commercial Life*, pp. 148–185. London: Sage.

Merrifield, Andy (2000) 'Henri Lefebvre: A socialist in space'. In Michael Crang & Nigel Thrift (eds.), *Thinking Space*. London: Routledge.

Meyer, Birgit & Pels, Peter (2003) *Magic and Modernity: Interfaces of Revelation and Concealment*. Stanford: Stanford University Press.

Miller, Daniel (1998a) *A Theory of Shopping*. Ithaca: Cornell University Press.

Miller, Daniel (1998b) 'Why Some Things Matter'. In id., *Material Cultures. Why Some Things Matter*, pp. 3–24. Chicago: Chicago University Press.

Miller, Daniel (2001) 'Possessions'. In id., (ed.), *Home Possessions: Material Culture behind Closed Doors*, pp. 107–121. Oxford: Berg.

Moran, Joe. 2007. *Queuing for Beginners: The Story of Daily Life from Breakfast to Bedtime*. London: Profile Books.

Mossberg, Lena & Nissen Johansen, Erik (2006) *Storytelling: Marknadsföring i upplevelseindustrin*. Lund: Studentlitteratur.

Mullins, Laurie J. (2001) *Hospitality Management and Organisational Behaviour*. Essex: Pearson Educational Limited.

Nestius, Nenne (2006) 'Välkommen och njut av Spa & Hälsa', *Spa & hälsa* 1: p. 4.

New Shorter Oxford English Dictionary on Historical Principles (1993) Lesley Brown (ed.), Volume 1, A–M. Oxford: Clarendon Press.

Nippert-Eng, Christena E. (1995) *Home and Work: Negotiating Boundaries through Everyday Life*. Chicago: University of Chicago Press.

Nordgren, Malin (2004) 'Många längtar efter kravlös beröring', *Dagens Nyheter* Insidan, April 1: p. 9.

Norlind, Tobias (1902) *Korta anteckningar ur Ramlösa brunns historia*. Helsingborg: Helsingborgs Typografiska Anstalt.

Nørretranders, Tor (1998) *The User Illusion: Cutting Consciousness Down to Size*. New York: Penguin Books.

O'Dell, Tom (2002) 'Etnicitet i spänningsfältet mellan kultur och biologi'. In Finnur Magnússon (ed.), *Etniska relationer i vård och omsorg*, pp. 17–60. Lund: Studentlitteratur.

O'Dell, Tom (2004) 'Cultural Kinesthesis', *Ethnologia Scandinavica* 34: pp. 108–129.

O'Dell, Tom (2005a) 'Experiencescapes: Blurring Borders and Testing Connections'. In Tom O'Dell & Peter Billing (eds.), *Experiencescapes: Tourism, Culture, and Economy*, pp. 11–33. Copenhagen: Copenhagen Business School Press.

O'Dell, Tom (2005b) 'Meditation, Magic, and Spiritual Regeneration: Spas and the Mass Production of Serenity', in Orvar Löfgren & Robert Willim (eds.), *Magic, Culture, and the New Economy*, pp. 19–36. Oxford: Berg.

O'Dell, Tom (2005c) 'To Haunt and Enthrall: The Cultural Kinesthetics of Minds and Bodies', *Ethnologia Scandinavica* 35: pp. 21–24.

O'Dell, Tom (2005d) 'Management Strategies and the Need for Fun'. In Tom O'Dell

& Peter Billing (eds.), *Experiencescapes: Tourism, Culture & Economy*, pp. 127–144. Copenhagen: Copenhagen Business School Press.

O'Dell, T. (2006) 'Magic, Health and the Mediation of the Body's Geography'. In J. Falkheimer & A. Jansson (eds.), *Geographies of Communication. The Spatial Turn in Media Studies*, pp. 219–237. Gothenburg: Nordicom.

O'Dell, Tom (2007a) 'Tourist Experiences and Academic Junctures', *Scandinavian Journal of Hospitality and Tourism* 7(1): pp. 34–45.

O'Dell, Tom (2007b) 'Hospitality, Kinesthesis, and Health: Swedish Spas and the Market for Well-Being'. In Jennie Germann Molz & Sarah Gibson (eds.), *Mobilizing Hospitality*, pp. 103–120. London: Ashgate.

O'Dell, Tom & Billing, Peter (2005) *Experiencescapes: Tourism, Culture & Economy*. Copenhagen: Copenhagen Business School Press.

Peiss, Kathy (1986) *Cheap Amusements: Working Women and Leisure in Turn-of-the-Century New York*. Philadelphia: Temple University Press.

Pels, Peter (2003) 'Spirits of Modernity: Alfred Wallace, Edward Tylor, and the Visual Politics of Fact', in Birgit Meyer & Peter Pels (eds.), *Magic and Modernity: Interfaces of Revelation and Concealment*, pp. 241–271. Stanford: Stanford University Press.

Peters, Tom (1994) *The Pursuit of WOW! Every Person's Guide to Topsy-Turvy Times*. New York: Vintage Books.

Pettersson, Charlotte (1999) 'Njut av badrumslyx', *Sköna hem* 9: pp. 58–61.

Pine, Joseph & Gilmore, James (1998) 'Welcome to the Experience Economy', *Harvard Business Review* July–August: pp. 97–105.

Pine, Joseph & Gilmore, James (1999) *The Experience Economy: Work is Theatre & Every Business a Stage*. Boston: Harvard Business School Press.

Ramberg, Klas (2004) 'Ut ur skiten! Om hygien i folkhemmets bostadsfråga'. In Christina Westergren (ed.), *Tio tvättar sig*, pp. 109–132. Stockholm: Nordiska museets förlag.

Ramlösa Brunns- och Badtidning (1882) 'Anmälde gäster den 21 maj 1882', Sunday May 21, 1882: 1.

Ramlösa Hallået (1899) 'Hallå! Hallå!', *Ramlösa Hallået* 1899: 5.

Ramlösa Hallået (1912) 'Program för pingstfestligheterna i Ramlösa Brunn'. *Ramlösa Hallået* 1912: 7.

Ray, Larry & Sayer, Andrew (1999) *Culture and Economy After the Cultural Turn*. London: Sage.

Ridderstråle, Jonas & Nordström, Kjell (2002) *Funky Business: Talent Makes Capital Dance*. London: Pearson Education.

Ristilammi, Per-Markku (2002) 'Ballonger och fantomkänslor'. In Per Olof Berg, Anders Linde-Laursen, Orvar Löfgren (eds.), *Öresundsbron på uppmärkamhetens marknad: Regionbyggare i evenemangsbranschen*, pp. 115–126. Lund: Studentlitteratur.

Sandoval-Strausz, A.K. (2007) *Hotel: An American History*. New Haven: Yale University Press.

Sanova advertisement (2005) *Konstvärlden & [disajn]* 6: p. 63.

Schrage, Michael (1999) *Serious Play: How the World's Best Companies Simulate to Innovate*. Cambridge: Harvard Business School Press.

Selwyn, Tom (2000) 'An anthropology of hospitality'. In Conrad Lashley & Alison Morrison (eds.), *In Search of Hospitality: Theoretical Perspectives and Debates*, pp. 18–37. Oxford: Butterworth-Heinemann.

Sennett, Richard (1998) *The Corrosion of Character: The Personal Consequences of Work in the New Capitalism*. New York: W.W. Norton & Company.

Sennett, Richard (1999) 'Growth and Failure: The New Political Economy and its

Culture'. In Mike Featherstone & Scott Lasch (eds.), *Spaces of Culture: City, Nation, World*, pp. 14–26. London: Sage.

Sensa Spa brochure (2003) Lund: Sensa Spa.

Shove, Elizabeth (2003) *Comfort, Cleanliness and Convenience: The Social Organization of Normality*. Oxford: Berg.

Slyomovics, Susan (1993) 'The Body in Water: Women in American Spa Culture'. In Katherine Young (ed.), *Bodylore*. Knoxville: The University of Tennessee Press.

Smith, Benjamin Richard (2007) 'Body, Mind and Spirit? Towards an Analysis of the Practice of Yoga', *Body & Society* 13(2): pp. 25–46.

Soja, Edward (1996) *Thirdspace: Journeys to Los Angeles and Other Real-And-Imagined Places*. Malden: Blackwell Publications.

Spa Magazine (2002) 'Själen i japansk källa', *Spa Magazine* 1: pp. 25–27.

Stacey, Jackie (2000) 'The Global Within: Consuming Nature, Embodying Health'. In Sarah Franklin, Celia Lury & Jackie Stacey (eds.), *Global Nature, Global Culture*, pp. 97–145. London: SAGE Publications.

Strandberg, Lina (2004) 'Händer som kan ge patienter lugn och lindring', *Dagens Nyheter* Insidan, March 25: pp. 14–15.

Strang, Veronica (2004) *The Meaning of Water*. Oxford: Berg.

Svensk hotellrevy (2003) 'Arbetsvillkor, problem och krav på 5 av landets spa-ställen', 6–7: pp. 22–23.

Swanberg, Lena Katarina (2001) 'Spa en lustresa', *Sköna hem* 12: pp. 113–116.

Tacchi, Jo (1998) 'Radio Texture: Between Self and Others', In Daniel Miller (ed.), *Material Cultures: Why Some Things Matter*, pp. 25–46. Chicago: University of Chicago Press.

Taussig, Michael (1993) *Mimesis and Alterity: A Particular History of the Senses*. New York: Routledge.

Taylor, Bev (2001) 'The effects of Healing Touch, on the coping ability, self esteem and general health of undergraduate nursing students', *Complementary Therapies in Nursing & Midwifery* 7: pp. 34–42.

Telfer, Elisabeth (2000) 'The Philosophy of Hospitableness'. In Conrad Lashley & Alison Morrison (eds.), *In Search of Hospitality: Theoretical Perspectives and Debates*, pp. 38–55. Oxford: Butterworth-Heinemann.

Testa, Mark & Sipe, Lori (2006) 'A Systems Approach to Service Quality: Tools For Hospitality Leaders', *Cornell Hotel and Restaurant Administration Quarterly* 47(1): pp. 36–48.

Thornberg, Harald (1899) 'Barmhertighet'. *Ramlösa-Hallået* 1: 1.

Thrift, Nigel (1996) *Spatial Formations*. London: Sage Publications.

Thrift, Nigel (2000a) 'Performing Cultures in the New Economy'. *Annals of the Association of American Geographers* 90(4): pp. 674–692.

Thrift, Nigel (2000b) 'Still Life in Nearly Present Time: The Object of Nature', *Body & Society* 3–4: pp. 34–57.

Thrift, Nigel (2004) 'Intensities of Feeling: Towards a Spatial Politics of Affect', *Geografiska Annaler* 86(1): pp. 57–78.

Tryggstad, Lena (undated) 'Ett möte en chans'. In Kerstin Kåll (ed.), *Yasuragi: Stillhet, skönhet, harmoni*, pp. 4–7. Stockholm: Bokförlaget Fischer & Co.

Tylö advertisement (1968) 'Nu badar min fru också bastu…', *Allt i Hemmet* 3: 72.

Varbergs Kurort Hotell & Spa (undated) brochure. Varberg: Varbergs Kurort Hotel & Spa.

Varbergs Kurort Hotell & Spa (2002). Varberg: Varbergs Kurort Hotel & Spa.

Varbergs Kurort brochure (2006). Varberg: Varbergs Kurort Hotel & Spa.

Varbergs Stadshotell & Asia Spa brochure (2006) *Leva Möta Vila*. Varberg: Varbergs Stadshotell & Asia Spa.

Venn, Couze (2002) 'Altered States: Post-Enlightenment Cosmopolitanism and Trans-modern Socialities', *Theory, Culture & Society* 19(1–2): pp. 65–80

Vi i Villa (2008) 'Villaägarnas våta dröm är klinkers och jacuzzi', http://www.viivvilla. se/41857.aspx>, accessed on February 25, 2008.

Vik, Kajsa (1995) *Varberg Kurort Apelviken*. Varberg: Kurortens samfällighetsförening.

Walton, John (2000) 'The hospitality trades: a social history'. In Conrad Lashley & Alison Morrison (eds.), *In Search of Hospitality: Theoretical Perspectives and Debates*. pp. 56–76. Oxford: Butterworth-Heinemann.

Webster's New World Dictionary (1986) New York: Prentice Hall Press.

Weiner, Margaret (2003) 'Hidden Forces: Colonialism and the Politics of Magic'. In Birgit Meyer & Peter Pels (eds.), *Magic and Modernity: Interfaces of Revelation and Concealment*, pp. 129–58. Stanford: Stanford University Press.

Weisz, George (2001) 'Spas, Mineral Water, and Hydrological Science in Twentieth-Century France', *Isis* 92 (3): pp. 451–483.

Willim, Robert (2002) *Framtid.nu: Flyt och friktion i ett snabbt företag*. Stockholm/Stehag: Brutus Östlings Bokförlag Symposion.

Wolff, Janet (1995) *Resident Alien: Feminist Cultural Criticism*. Cambridge: Polity Press.

Wood, Roy (1994) 'Hotel Culture and Social Control', *Annals of Tourism Research* 21: pp. 65–80.

Woods, Robert (1991) 'Hospitality's History: Who Wrote What About When', *The Cornell H.R.A. Quarterly* August: pp. 89–95.

Yasuragi brochure *Sinnesro* (undated). Hasseludden: Yasuragi Hasseludden.

Ystads Saltjöbad brochure (2005). Ystad: Ystads Saltsjöbad.

Zernike, Kate (2005) 'The Spa-ification of America', *The New York Times* January 2, Section 5(1): pp. 8–9.

Žižek, Slavoj (1997) *The Plague of Fantasies*. London: Verso.

Internet sources

<www.amazon.com/Scientific-Explorers-Spa-Science-Chemistry/dp/B0006OHMU6/ ref=pd_sim_t_title_1>, accessed February 22, 2008.

<www.discoverspas.com/ne>, accessed August 21, 2007.

<ws/newsstudies7.shtml>, accessed August 21, 2007.

<www.discoverspas.com/news/newsstudies7.shtml>, accessed August 21, 2007

<www.discoverspas.com/news/newsevents114.shtml>, accessed August 21, 2007.

<www.google.se/search?q=hospitality&hl=sv&lr=&start=0&sa=N>, accessed November 8, 2006.

<www.hasseludden.com>, accessed 2003-09-02 & September 24, 2007.

, accessed November 8, 2006.

<www.hotels-weekly.com> 'News & Analysis'. 'Spa Hyatt Leads the Way', accessed September 2, 2003.

<www.traveldailynews.com/makeof.asp?central_id=521&permanent_id=17>, accessed August 22, 2007.

<www.viivilla.se/41857.aspx>, accessed February 25, 2008.

<www.yasuragi.se/info.asp/id/152516>, accessed July 3, 2007.